LEONARD LEE RUE III'S

Way of the Whitetail

Dr. Leonard Lee Rue III

Voyageur Press

Edited by Amy Rost-Holtz
Designed by Andrea Rud
Printed in Hong Kong

00   01   02   03   04   5   4   3   2

Library of Congress Cataloging-in-Publication Data
Rue, Leonard Lee.
    Leonard Lee Rue III's way of the whitetail / Leonard Lee Rue III.
      p. cm.
    Includes bibliographical references (p. 154).
    ISBN 0-89658-417-8
    1. White-tailed deer—Behavior. I. Title.

  QL737.U55 R837 2000
  599.65'215—dc21   00-024654

Distributed in Canada by Raincoast Books, 9050 Shaughnessy Street, Vancouver, B.C. V6P 6E5

Published by Voyageur Press, Inc.
123 North Second Street, P.O. Box 338, Stillwater, MN 55082 U.S.A.
651-430-2210, fax 651-430-2211
books@voyageurpress.com
www.voyageurpress.com

Educators, fundraisers, premium and gift buyers, publicists, and marketing managers: Looking for creative products and new sales ideas? Voyageur Press books are available at special discounts when purchased in quantities, and special editions can be created to your specifications. For details contact the marketing department at 800-888-9653.

On the frontispiece: *The hugely swollen neck is indicative of a dominant whitetail at the peak of the rut. (Leonard Lee Rue III)*

On the title page: *A sight seldom seen—four trophy bucks together, crossing a Louisiana bayou. (Len Rue, Jr.)*

Facing page: *Many Texas bucks have large bodies as well as large antlers. (Len Rue, Jr.)*

DEDICATION

This book is dedicated to my five "adopted" sons:

Len Clifford
Mike Keating
Rod Parsons
Mike Roberts
Gene Stires

ACKNOWLEDGMENTS

Mine is empirical knowledge gained from the countless thousands upon thousands of hours that I have spent observing, studying, hunting, and photographing deer. The "Dr." before my name is an honorary title given to me by Colorado State University "for the dissemination of knowledge." I have not had the biological training, nor access to laboratories, to carry out the exacting scientific experiments and studies to document the internal and chemical responses in the behavior of deer. For that I have had to go to the work and papers of the many top deer research biologists and zoologists, such as Thomas Atkeson, Anthony A. Bubenik, G. A. Bubenik, Gary L. Doster, David C. Guyn, D. G. Hirth, Harry Jacobson, Kent E. Kammermeyer, James C. Kroll, R. Larry Marchinton, Karl V. Miller, D. Muller-Schwarze, John Ozoga, Louis Verme, and many, many more. These are men whose work I greatly respect, and I feel privileged to be able to call some of them friends. Three of these men, Harry Jacobson, Larry Marchinton, and John Ozoga, were kind enough to read and review my entire manuscript and offer their suggestions and corrections. For that I am truly thankful. Their contributions have made this a better book. John Ozoga has also written the foreword.

Special thanks goes to Rod Parsons for sharing his knowledge, to Kurt von Besser of Atsko, Inc. for allowing me to use his charts on what a deer sees, and to Mark Stallings for providing the deer accident charts and statistics.

My thanks to my secretary, Marilyn Maring, for her help on my manuscript and for doing the typing. Thanks also to my son, Len Rue, Jr., whose many photos help to enhance this book, and for all the fun we have had over all the miles and years getting them.

My heartfelt thanks to Amy Rost-Holtz, my editor at Voyageur Press. Her many suggestions made this a better book. She was a pleasure to work with.

Last, but definitely not the least, my thanks to my lovely wife, Uschi, for the use of her photos and for her constant help and support in everything that I do.

Dr. Leonard Lee Rue III

Cautious but confident, this buck is on the move looking for estrus does. (Len Rue, Jr.)

CONTENTS

In proving his superiority, this battle-scarred whitetail buck has broken one of his antler tines. (Len Rue, Jr.)

FOREWORD

By John J. Ozoga

TODAY THE INCREDIBLY ADAPTIVE WHITE-TAILED DEER IS ONE OF THE MOST CONTROVERSIAL mammals on the North American continent. We have made great strides in deer management, and informed and educated hunters, as well as non-hunters, are an integral part of any deer management program. But without public understanding and support, even the most profound deer management agenda is destined to fail. Implementation of biologically sound practices can be easily short-stopped by a naïve public, especially when public opinion is fueled by misinformation from an ecologically ignorant press.

I suspect Dr. Leonard Lee Rue III has done more to educate the American public about the true ways of the whitetail than anyone. He has communicated basic deer biology—through his writing, photographs and lectures—long before such information was fashionable in popular literature. And he continues to do so with gusto, enviable enthusiasm, new insights, and remarkable success, as evidenced in this, his latest book, *Leonard Lee Rue III's Way of the Whitetail.*

Rue is not your "run-of-the-mill" outdoor writer, as one could judge when Colorado State University bestowed upon him an honorary doctorate degree, as recognition for his efforts to educate the general public. In addition to being a top-notch communicator, he is an astute observer with an inquisitive mind. And he has long-term experience with the whitetail—which, in itself, is not so common among biologists these days. This broad experience, plus his communicative skills, allows him to put together a story of whitetail behavior few others would even dare attempt.

When I started as a wildlife research biologist, some thirty-eight years ago, I was especially interested in the social behavior of whitetails, which was then poorly understood and considered a subject of little more than academic importance. With the recent interest in Quality Deer Management, however, and the associated emphasis on maintaining deer populations in social balance, as well as nutritional balance, a firm understanding of whitetail behavioral patterns takes on new importance.

Exertion, stress, or heat will cause a deer to breathe through its mouth. (Len Rue, Jr.)

To his credit, Rue carefully blends his own observational information with information documented in scientific literature. He is forever questioning what he sees, as well as what has previously been reported as "gospel." If he can't provide a reasonable explanation for unique events, he'll search out those who have studied such things in detail and pick their brains. The result is new factual information to increase our understanding of this very "plastic," ever-changing, highly adaptive species, the white-tailed deer.

The information in this book is not a rehash of existing knowledge—it's strikingly new. In Rue's traditional style, this book contains something I refer to as "soft science": It's scientifically sound, but it's an easy read, without all the technical jargon and statistics characteristic of science journal articles.

Follow the whitetail's behavior through the seasons—month by month—and learn how such a forest-dwelling animal uses its senses to survive in a hostile world, while employing glandular secretions as its primary mode of communication.

Winter is a season of hardship for whitetails throughout much of their range. To survive, they must be physically well prepared and then become ultra-energy-conservative. In the north, it's a time of cold and snow, and of limited food, when hundreds of thousands of whitetails can die. Even in the south, however, drought, floods, or other unusual weather patterns during summer and autumn can set the stage for sizable malnutrition-calculated whitetail losses during the winter season. In any case, winter is a time when the sinister grim reaper takes its toll, but the superior animals somehow manage to survive.

Springtime can provide whitetails with the most favorable, but sometimes the toughest environmental conditions the species is likely to experience. A delayed spring may cause catastrophic mortality in the north, but an early green-up will provide whitetails with an abundance of highly nutritious forage. Spring is when the fawns are born, when the nursing doe becomes an aggressive beast, and when adult bucks seek peace and solitude to grow their new crowns of antlers.

Summer is a tranquil season for whitetails, if there is such a time for any prey species. For most whitetails, it is a season of plenty. It is a comparatively brief period, when the tentative doe with fawns is a virtual milk-producing machine and when the young grow and learn. Summer is also when bucks replace spent body tissues, begin to build fat stores for the rut, and put the final touch on their new antlers.

The shortening days of autumn set in motion a host of physiological changes that determine whether the species will flourish or flounder. Autumn is, without doubt, the whitetail's most hectic season. It is socially, physiologically, and nutritionally complex. This is when bucks establish dominance hierarchies, make prominent "signposts," communicate their status to prospective mates, and breed—all within the matter of a couple of months. And at this time all deer fatten

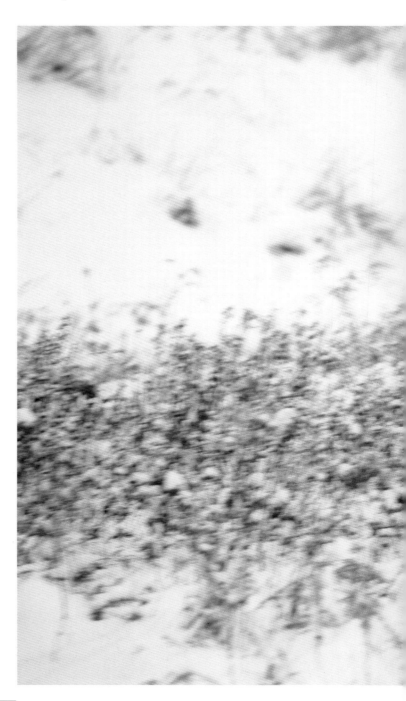

for the coming winter. Then the cycle starts all over again.

Rue leads you through the whitetail's seasonal cycle with detail, accuracy, and intrigue. You will soon realize how versatile and adaptive this creature is and begin to appreciate how this one species can occupy such a vast geographic range, and even expand that range, while many other species of wildlife struggle to merely exist in the presence of humans. If you are not currently a devoted fan of the white-tailed deer, I wager you will be after reading this book.

C. W. Severinghaus, a New York state deer researcher, measured one buck's jump, going slightly downhill, at twenty-nine feet. (Len Rue, Jr.)

INTRODUCTION

IT WAS ONE OF THOSE DAYS THAT YOU NEVER FORGET—A GORGEOUS SPRING MORNING IN early June 1939. I had just walked the cows down to the back pasture and was heading back to the house for breakfast. The "bob-bob-white" of a male quail calling from the fencerow lured me from the lane, and I was tip-toeing along the edge of the cornfield.

Suddenly I saw it in among the rows of the green, newly sprouted corn spires. Pressed quite deeply into the soft brown earth was the elongated heart-shaped impression. Then I saw another, and another, and another. The quail was forgotten. All of my attention was focused on those impressions. Being a student of Ernest Thompson Seton's books on wildlife, I knew instantly that what I was looking at were the tracks of a white-tailed deer, the first tracks of a white-tailed deer I had ever seen. That deer had actually walked across our field; that meant it might still be in the vicinity, and, although it probably was, I didn't see it that morning. I began seeing deer tracks more frequently, but I didn't see my first deer for another two months. It was three and one-half years before I shot my first deer, a small four-point buck, in December 1942.

It's hard to describe the elation I felt upon seeing that first deer track. New Jersey was just recovering from the almost complete annihilation of the white-tailed deer in the state. In the late 1800s, Whitmer Stone of the Pennsylvania Wildlife Museum thought that there were probably fewer than two hundred deer left in all of New Jersey. He recommended that some of the skins and skulls of these deer be preserved in New Jersey's State Museum so future generations would have a record of the deer that had once inhabited the state. In 1897, Samuel Rhodes wrote that "deer had long since been exterminated in northern New Jersey." And New Jersey was not alone. At the turn of the century, it was estimated that there were fewer than five hundred thousand deer left on the entire North American continent, north of the Mexican border.

It's a heart-stopping moment when a huge buck like this steps out of the shadows. (Len Rue, Jr.)

Today the number of whitetails for that same area numbers up to twenty million animals—one of conservation's greatest success stories. In fact, in many areas, we have too many deer. We have moved from complete protection, through "bucks only" laws, to emphasis on the heavy harvesting of does in an effort to curb the herds. We no longer talk about the carrying capacity of the land, because that has long since been exceeded; we now have to deal with the social carrying capacity—the wants and needs of the land-owners and the public at large. The general public has gone from believing in the Bambi syndrome (we love them all) to taking the NIMBY position (we still love them all, but Not In My Backyard).

Unlike Europe, where most of the game belongs to the land owners, in North America the game belongs to the states and provinces and is a trust held for the general public, even when the bulk of the wildlife lives on private land. Most state game departments are funded solely by the license fees from hunters, and the original goal of the game departments was to provide as much game for the hunters as was possible. Today the game departments have to consider not only the desires of the hunter, but the social carrying capacity as well.

Whereas most hunters today want even more deer, many states have been forced into the position of having to cut back on their deer herds, and they are doing this by extending the seasons and increasing the take. In the fall of 1998, Dan Ferrigno, deer project leader for New Jersey's Division of Fish, Game and Wildlife said, "In certain deer management areas, if you took every animal the regulations allowed you to, your season limit would be 119 deer." And, again, New Jersey is not alone. Many states offer unlimited deer hunting opportunities.

This era is America's "Golden Age" for the white-tailed deer. Richard McCabe and Richard E. McCabe figured that there were between twenty-four to thirty-three million white-tailed deer in North America in pre-Columbian times, but our deer population today is the highest it has been since the mid-1600s. A burgeoning human population and the destruction of habitat means that the number of deer will have to be reduced. However, better management and our ever increasing knowledge of the deer themselves should make sure that the deer's future is assured. They have come into the twenty-first century, with us, in good shape.

A powerful young buck takes flight. (Len Rue, Jr.)

It is because of our ever increasing knowledge that this book is written. I wrote *The World of the White-tailed Deer* in 1962, and sixteen years later I wrote *The Deer of North America*. In 1989, I revised the latter book to include the wealth of new information I had gained in the intervening eleven years, and that revised edition was reissued in 1998. The basic information has not been changed because it did not need to be. This book will complement that volume because it stresses the area in which we have gained so much new knowledge about the behavior of deer. In its broadest sense, the behavior of a species is the action or reaction—autonomic, innate, or learned—within itself or to conspecifics, to other species, and to its environment. That's what this book is about.

Above: *The heart-shaped hoofed footprint of the white-tailed deer in newly sprouted corn. (Leonard Lee Rue III)*

Right: *We just don't know all the reasons why some bucks have non-typical antlers. (Len Rue, Jr.)*

PART I

The Essential Whitetail

This buck froze in mid-stride at the sounds of the camera's shutter clicking. (Len Rue, Jr.)

Chapter One

THE WHITE-TAILED DEER

THERE ARE THIRTY RECOGNIZED SUBSPECIES OF THE WHITE-TAILED DEER, WITH SEVENTEEN found in North America, north of the Mexican border. When I say "recognized," I mean that taxonomists (biologists who scientifically classify, qualify, and identify all living creatures) tell us that there are seventeen types of North American white-tailed deer that are sufficiently different from each other that they deserve their own subspecies classification. The taxonomists tell us this because most of us, and perhaps I should say all of us except for the taxonomists, cannot tell most of the subspecies apart. Prior to the advent of DNA testing, subspeciation was based on the deer's body size and skull differences and where the deer were found because, in some instances, there was spatial isolation.

No one has any trouble seeing the obvious difference in the body size and the antler development between most of the northern deer and the southern deer. Natural selection, producing the different subspecies, is governed by four biological laws. Bergmann's Rule, the most important, states that the farther north or south of the equator a species is found, the larger its body will be. Larger bodies have smaller surface areas in relation to their actual weight, which conserves body heat. Conversely, the hotter the habitat, the smaller the species' body will be in relation to its surface area, allowing for greater heat dissipation.

A truly magnificent whitetail buck in mid-winter. (Len Rue, Jr.)

I have written "Rue's Rule," an amendment to Bergmann's Rule that reads, ". . . the larger the members of the same species will be, so long as their preferred food is abundant and meets their nutritional needs." Body size decreases in direct proportion to decreasing food supplies. This second biological law can be seen in the smaller size of the Peary's caribou.

The third biological law, Allen's Rule, states that among warm-blooded creatures, the physical extremities—ears, tail, and legs—are shorter in the cooler part of their range than in the warmer part. This rule is borne out by the Coues whitetail (*Odocoileus virginianus couesi*) of southern Arizona, which has larger ears and tail relative to body size than the northern deer. When hunters or other observers see the relatively mule-eared Coues deer (also known as the Arizona whitetail) at a distance, they occasionally mistake it for a mule deer. Nevertheless, the color and shape of the tail and, in a mature buck, the conformation of the antlers will usually distinguish a subspecies of this whitetail from a muley where both species are encountered. (In subse-quent pages, I will give detailed descriptions to facilitate field identification.)

The fourth law, Gloger's Rule, states that among warm-blooded animals, dark pigments are most prevalent in warm, humid habitat. I must add that dark coloration also tends to prevail in forested regions. Note that the darkness depends on humidity as well as temperature. Hot, dry habitat does not produce dark coloration, for pigment is a survival factor, and a dark deer (or other prey species) would invite predation by standing out conspicuously against a background of desert rock and sand. Red and yellow tints tend to dominate in arid regions, and paler tones—reduced pigmentation—dominate in colder climates. You will see the operation of Gloger's Rule in the descriptions of the various subspecies.

Our most southern deer, Florida's Key Deer (*O. v. clavium*) is our smallest subspecies. A big Key deer buck may stand twenty-eight inches high at the shoulder and weigh up to 80 pounds, but most are much smaller. Large specimens of our three largest subspecies, the

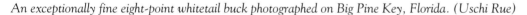

An exceptionally fine eight-point whitetail buck photographed on Big Pine Key, Florida. (Uschi Rue)

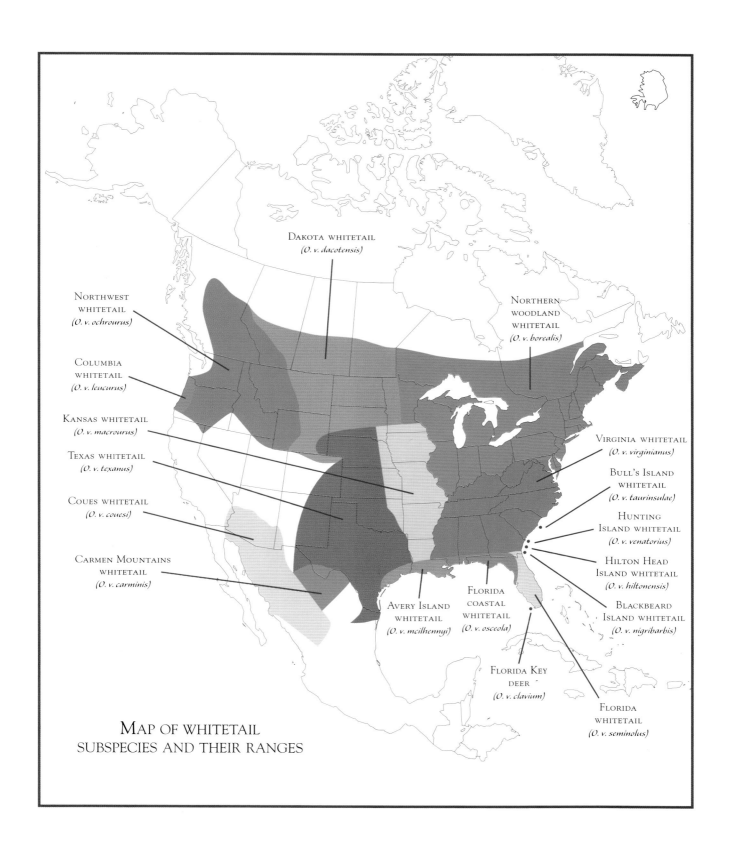

NORTHWEST
WHITETAIL
(O. v. ochrourus)

COLUMBIA
WHITETAIL
(O. v. leucurus)

KANSAS WHITETAIL
(O. v. macrourus)

TEXAS WHITETAIL
(O. v. texanus)

COUES WHITETAIL
(O. v. couesi)

CARMEN MOUNTAINS
WHITETAIL
(O. v. carminis)

DAKOTA WHITETAIL
(O. v. dacotensis)

NORTHERN
WOODLAND
WHITETAIL
(O. v. borealis)

VIRGINIA WHITETAIL
(O. v. virginianus)

BULL'S ISLAND
WHITETAIL
(O. v. taurinsulae)

HUNTING
ISLAND WHITETAIL
(O. v. venatorius)

HILTON HEAD
ISLAND WHITETAIL
(O. v. hiltonensis)

BLACKBEARD
ISLAND WHITETAIL
(O. v. nigribarbis)

AVERY ISLAND
WHITETAIL
(O. v. mcilhennyi)

FLORIDA
COASTAL
WHITETAIL
(O. v. osceola)

FLORIDA KEY
DEER
(O. v. clavium)

FLORIDA
WHITETAIL
(O. v. seminolus)

MAP OF WHITETAIL
SUBSPECIES AND THEIR RANGES

Above: *A big eight-point* Borealis *whitetail buck. (Uschi Rue)*

Facing page: *A big-antlered, big-bodied Texas whitetail buck. (Uschi Rue)*

northern woodland whitetails (*O. v. borealis*), the Dakota whitetail (*O. v. dakotensis*), and the northwest whitetail (*O. v. ochrourus*), stand about thirty-eight to forty-one inches high at the shoulder and weigh between 200 and 400 pounds. Two Minnesota bucks had generally estimated live weights of 512 pounds, based on the actual scale weights of their dressed carcasses. However, the conversion rates are not as accurate on large deer as small ones because large deer lose a smaller percentage of weight when dressed.

Among all of, and within, the various subspecies, there is a tremendous variation in the actual body size, weight, and antler development, due to age, genetics, herd composition, soil fertility, weather, and the supply of nutritious food available to that individual animal.

On parts of the Edwards Plateau in central Texas, where there are more than one hundred deer to the square mile, the deer are not much bigger than goats. The small size of these Texas whitetails (*O. v. Texanus*) is primarily due to overpopulation, poor soils, and drought conditions. The Carmen Mountain whitetails (*O. v. carminis*), small deer to start with, are smaller in size. This isolated subspecies is found primarily in the Big Bend area of Texas and is separated from the Texas whitetail by a buffer strip of semi-desert, which is home to desert mule deer. However, the Texas whitetail is expanding its range and interbreeding with the mule deer, as will be discussed later.

Although the deer of Texas are smaller than the deer of the northern United States and Canada, I have seen some really big-bodied deer as far south as the Rio Grande—deer that rivaled the northern deer in antler size, but not in weight. It has always been acknowledged that some of the Texas bucks had really large antlers that appeared to be even larger than they actually were because of the small body size of the deer.

What I am saying is that I have seen deer that had not only large antlers, but large bodies as well. How did that happen?

There are several reasons. The first is the principle of "you are what you eat." Most men today could not fit in the suits of armor the knights wore seven hundred years ago; we are much too big. According to the U.S. Army, our soldiers of today are two to three inches taller than were the soldiers in World War I. The best example is how much taller than their parents the young Japanese are today. This increased body size in humans is the result of better, more nutritious, higher protein diets. The same is true of deer. At all of the ranches where I photograph, they feed the deer constantly, and this is increasing the deer's body size.

The second reason, and this is true of deer all over the country, is that there has been such a transporting of deer from one section of the country to another that most subspeciation does not hold up any longer,

as mentioned in my first paragraph in this chapter. For example, the deer in my area, New Jersey, had been completely wiped out. Our present herd owes its existence mainly to the owners of the Rutherford Estate in Allamuchy and the Worthington Estate near the Delaware Water Gap. Both of these estates had large deer parks, populated with deer they had imported from Michigan and Wisconsin. The Worthington Estate had a sixteen strand barbed wire fence enclosure ten miles long. The fence was built in 1889 and patrolled daily by a game keeper. In spite of private hunting and the sale of surplus animals, the deer herd grew so large so fast that, by 1911, the fenced-in area was doubled.

In 1904, the New Jersey Board of Fish and Game Commissions purchased one hundred deer from the Worthingtons and distributed them throughout the state. In 1911, the Commission released forty-seven more whitetails they purchased from Michigan. A few years later the Worthingtons removed most of their

A whitetail doe feeding in Florida's Everglades. (Leonard Lee Rue III)

The Dakota whitetails of Montana are also large deer. (Leonard Lee Rue III)

fences and allowed their deer to spill out to populate the surrounding areas. It is from this nucleus, and escapees from the Rutherford Estate, that the deer in northern New Jersey and eastern Pennsylvania were established.

This scenario has been repeated in state after state as each tried to re-establish their own deer herds. The deer that were brought into New Jersey were *O. v. borealis*, the same subspecies originally found in the state. Most of the other states imported subspecies that were different from those originally found there. This is particularly true of Texas where many ranchers, whose deer bring in more money than cattle, stocked northern deer to increase the size of their local deer. The ranchers realized that bringing in one buck as a one shot deal wouldn't work because the northern buck's genes would be diluted to the point of almost non-existence in just four generations. Where both northern bucks and does were imported and released together, which is what most of the states did, their bloodlines were established, especially where no native deer were present. The original subspeciation of deer, which was designated by where the deer were found, has been subverted in most areas, as non-native deer flourished in their new locations.

Chapter Two

SENSES

To a greater or lesser extent, deer have the same five senses—sight, hearing, smell, taste, and touch—that so dominate our lives, and it is through these senses that they communicate.

SIGHT

Because we humans are basically a predator species, our eyes are located on the front of our heads, giving us binocular vision. Our range of vision covers about 170 degrees, with some of us having peripheral vision up to 180 degrees of a circle. Deer, being a prey species, have eyes situated on the sides of their heads, but their eyes are angled at about 25 degrees toward the nose. Deer can see about 310 degrees of a circle, most of which is monocular vision, although they do have an overlapping field in the front that gives them about 50 degrees of binocular vision.

While the pupil of a human's eye is round, that of a deer is rectangular. The curvature of a deer's eye bulges out about one-quarter inch beyond the skull. These are features that enhance its wide field of vision.

The fovea of a human eye allows us to have greater acuity and to see close objects with much greater sharpness. A deer's eye is geared to detect motion, the slightest motion, and to move while the subject is in the deer's range of vision is to ensure detection. To help to avoid detection, I wear Trebark camouflage, in one of its many seasonal patterns, at all times of the year when I am afield. Although many times I have not been identified by deer, even when caught out in the open, to be really successful in hunting, photographing, or just observing deer, you need to try to blend into the background. Deer so thoroughly know every feature of their home range that anything they see now that wasn't there before is suspect.

White-tailed deer constantly sniff the air currents for any tell-tale scent of danger. (Len Rue, Jr.)

While talking about wearing camouflage, it is important that you do not wash such clothing in any of the supermarket "super" detergents, because they all contain ultraviolet (UV) brighteners that not only makes your whites whiter than white, but makes your camo clothing brighter than bright. It has been discovered that deer can see the ultraviolet light emanating from clothing so washed. To prevent this, I wash all of my camo clothing in Sport Wash, produced by the Atsko/Sno-Seal Company of Orangeburg, South Carolina.

Deer have much larger eyes than humans do, and this allows for the transmittal of more light. The retina, the receptive surface at the back of the eye, is composed of rod and cone cells. Sharpness of vision and sensitivity to color depends on cone cells. We humans have more cones than rods. Rods are used primarily for night vision and deer have more rods. Behind the rods in many animals, including deer, is a reflective layer known as the tapetum, which passes the light back through the rods, doubling the amount of light the optic nerve receives. This produces the "eye shine" for which deer are famous. It has been calculated that deer can see at least one thousand times better than humans do in low light situations.

Extensive research has proven that deer can see in two different wavelengths of color. Deer have exceptionally good vision in the cold or blue range of the spectrum, and this allows them to see very well in extremely low light situations. They also can see the midrange spectrum of yellow. We humans see almost the entire spectrum of color in all the wavelengths, but the yellow filters in our eyes prevent us from seeing in the ultraviolet or extremely low light range.

As another aid to their vision, deer often use triangulation. Anyone who has been "discovered," but not identified, by a deer will have noticed the deer move its head either up or down or from side to side, thus giving its brain two vantage points of vision. This movement helps in depth perception and is an attempt to "flesh-out" the object being seen and perhaps identify it.

If you are attempting to stalk close to a deer, do so only while the deer has its head down feeding. At such times, the deer is preoccupied with what it will take in its mouth next. You can tell when the deer is about to raise its head because it almost always wags its tail before it does so. This is an involuntary action. How-

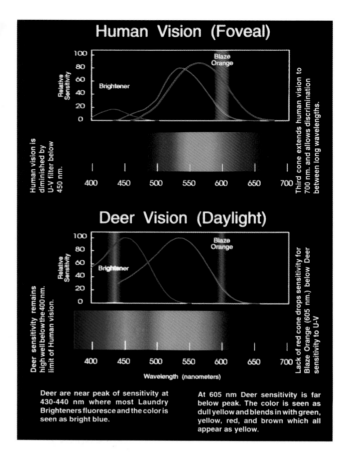

Colors appear differently to deer. UV colors are more prominent than other colors. (© Kurt von Besser, Atsko/Sno-Seal, Inc.)

Above: *A deer is at a disadvantage while it is actually feeding because it is focusing most of its attention on its next mouthful of food. (Len Rue, Jr.)*

Facing page: *A deer's eyes are located on the sides of the head, allowing it to see about 310 degrees of a circle. (Len Rue, Jr.)*

ever, if a deer is suspicious, it may use the diversionary tactic of pretending to feed without actually doing so. When it lowers its head, it is carefully monitoring its surroundings, not feeding. While employing this tactic, the deer does not wag its tail before raising its head.

HEARING

We humans often cup our hands behind our ears, which funnels more sound waves into the ear's auditory canal, allowing us to hear better. Deer don't have that problem; their ears are shaped like tapered flared funnels that move constantly, even while the deer is asleep. A whitetail's ear is about seven inches long by four and one-half inches at its widest point, giving it approximately twenty-four square inches of reflective surface. The auditory canal openings in a deer and a human are the same size, about one-third inch in diameter, but a deer's much larger ear allows more sound waves to be picked up and funneled.

Another advantage that deer have is that their range of hearing is much wider than humans'. Most human adults can hear frequencies in the range of forty to sixteen thousand cycles per second, with some people, especially children, hearing both lower and higher frequencies than is normal.

I know that deer can hear frequencies as high as thirty thousand cycles and perhaps beyond. I often use a "silent" dog whistle, while doing photography, to get a deer's attention and cause it to look at me alertly. These devices have been machine tested at thirty thousand cycles, and, although humans can't hear them, dogs and deer respond readily.

Under normal conditions deer, like humans, are able to filter out sounds that do not represent danger to them. Sounds that deer become accustomed to, such as acorns dropping, leaves being blown across the forest floor, tree branches rubbing together gently, traffic along a constantly used highway, and even the deafening noise of exploding shells on an artillery test range, are all sounds that deer become accustomed to and, as they don't represent danger, are filtered out and discounted. However, deer are extremely alert to the alarm notes given by any of the other creatures that share their environment. The clarion "PUUCK" of the wild turkey, the strident "CANT, CANT" of the blue jay, the "TSK, TSK, TSK" of an alarmed squirrel, the "CRACK" of a beaver's tail slap—all are made by the creatures in response to danger, and the deer

interpret those as such and are instantly alert.

Sometimes the greatest warning of danger is absolute silence. Usually a forest is quite a noisy place, and a constant barrage of familiar noise is the norm. When all creatures stop their activities and remain motionless and silent, they do so because of an imminent danger.

The most difficult time for deer, and for seeing deer, is during a period of high wind. When wind reaches a force of six on the Beaufort scale (twenty-two to twenty-seven miles per hour) and tree branches begin to crash together, the deer are as nervous as a cat on a hot tin roof. There is such a commotion going on that the deer cannot hear danger approaching and cannot smell it because the molecules of scent are almost instantly dissipated. At such times, the deer head for the most dense, remote cover in their area.

I often have said that a deer's ears are also directly linked to its "bump of curiosity." If the source of a sound cannot be confirmed by either sight or smell, it is usually investigated. I discovered this fact when I was about fifteen.

I was walking home one night around 11 P.M. without a flashlight. I was walking in a cut-bank lane, which meant I was about on eye level with the ground of the field on the uphill side. An explosive wheeze/snort startled me—and I do mean startled! Being lower than the field, I could make out three running deer outlined against the horizon. When they got about two hundred feet out, they stopped, and, because the wind was now angling in my favor, they couldn't smell me. As I didn't move, they didn't notice the top of my head. They should have been able to hear my heart pounding, but they didn't. They didn't just walk back; they came back in a cautious, rigid, foot-stomping gait. They didn't come back directly to me either, but circled until they caught my scent; then they were gone, their route marked with snorts at each jump.

SMELL

Of all the deer's senses, its sense of smell is the most important. That deer live in a world of scent has been proven time and time again by a deer's actions and reactions to scent. However, just what can a deer smell, and from how far away, are questions that can't be answered positively. Deer don't lend themselves to testing, as dogs do, because deer aren't at all interested in pleasing humans or working for a reward.

Above: *Whitetails are always very alert and very curious. (Leonard Lee Rue III)*

Left: *This doe's ears constantly sweep back and forth as she listens for danger. (Len Rue, Jr.)*

Above: *A deer always tries to confirm anything of which it is suspicious and uses its nose to positively identify new and unknown scents. (Leonard Lee Rue III)*

Facing page: *Frequent licking helps deer retain the moisture on their noses. (Leonard Lee Rue III)*

Most odors in the natural world are of organic compounds and are released as molecules of gas. For gases to be smelled, they must be dissolved or received in combination with moisture. An adult white-tailed buck's external nose has about three square inches of bare, moist surface that is used to trap scent molecules. In order to increase the efficiency of this surface, the deer frequently licks its nose with its tongue. The moist epithelial lining on the inside of the deer's nostrils is much larger than a human's; it traps scent molecules and contains the sensory nerve endings that lead to the two olfactory bulbs. A deer's olfactory bulbs also are much larger than those of a human's. The olfactory bulbs turn the chemical scent into electrical impulses that are sent to the brain's olfactory cortex, where the signals of the scent are classified. Scent is delivered to the olfactory bulbs not only through the nostrils but also through the open mouth via the nasopharynx (the throat). An animal usually sniffs the air in short drafts for a scent because the turbulence

set up in the nostrils increases the receptivity of the olfactory sensory nerve endings. (My wife said that I do the same thing, although I was not conscious of doing so until she mentioned it.)

Much has been written recently about the vomeronasal organ, two tiny pinpricks that reside in the top of a deer's palate about one inch from the front of its mouth. This organ is a counterpart to the Jacobsen's organ found in reptiles. The flicking of a snake's tongue is well known—it literally "tastes" everything in its world. In a deer, too, scent is brought in to the vomeronasal organ on the tongue or by air drawn in through the open mouth. The neurons of the vomeronasal organ do not go to the main olfactory bulb but to a separate, much smaller, accessory olfactory bulb and thence to an entirely different part of the brain. Its function also is much different. The main olfactory system elicits immediate response to feeling, fear, and behavioral, especially sexual, stimulants, while the vomeronasal system regulates the physiological readiness of the

Above: *A deer has a moist nose. The moisture aids the whitetail's sense of smell because it helps to trap scent molecules. The epithelial lining of a human's nose has about 10 million sensory cells, while that of a large dog has 220 million. Although it varies from compound to compound, research shows that an average dog's sense of smell is about two hundred times better than that of humans'. Deer probably have as many sensory cells as a dog, although I believe that a dog has a keener sense of smell than does a deer because the dog is a predator and tracks its prey while deer do not. (Len Rue, Jr.)*

Right: *This "deep-smelling" pose, done by all of the cloven-hoofed mammals, is known as flehmening. (Len Rue, Jr.)*

deer's system to breeding. Based on its exceedingly small size, compared to the large size of the deer's regular olfactory epithelium, the vomeronasal organ probably plays a minimal role in the deer's processing of scent. I bolster this view by pointing out that, at all times, the bulk of a deer's sniffing the air for scent molecules is done with its mouth closed, thus eliminating the vomeronasal organ of receiving any scent to process.

Most people are familiar with the deer's upper-lip curling action known as the flehmen. Although bucks flehmen throughout the year, they do it much more frequently during the rutting season when they are busy trying to identify other bucks by their urine or to check upon a doe's estrus status. The bucks flehmen after checking the doe's urine as she urinates, smelling the vegetation upon which drops of her urine may still cling, or smelling the ground which the doe or a rival buck has saturated with urine a short time before, yesterday, or even days earlier.

The deer's vomeronasal organs are located in the top of its mouth.
(Uschi Rue)

The vomeronasal organs of deer correspond to the Jacobsen's organ found in snakes. (Len Rue, Jr.)

The buck breathes in the scent molecules deeply, raises his muzzle high, and curls his upper lip, which closes his nostrils, locking the scent inside where it saturates the sensory nerve endings in the epithelial lining. While holding this position, he then exhales through his wide-open mouth, forcing some of the scent molecules past the vomeronasal organ.

Many variables, including wind, temperature, and moisture, affect the deer's ability to detect scent. High humidity, between 50 and 70 percent, with a temperature between fifty and seventy degrees Fahrenheit, and a light breeze make for ideal scenting conditions. Under such conditions I believe a deer could detect a human's scent from at least one-half mile or more.

Rain or snow knock scent molecules down and dissipate them. High temperatures cause thermals to lift scent molecules up and away. Cold and dampness negate scent as the molecules are hard to pick up in the cold, and, when the mucous linings of the deer's nostrils dry out, they are not as receptive.

It is interesting to note that a doe cannot recognize her own fawns by sight or the sound of their bleat. Fawns will nurse any doe that will allow it, but because a wild doe will allow only her own fawns to nurse, she has to check them by smelling them before allowing them to suckle.

TASTE

Of the deer's senses, taste probably plays the smallest role, yet it is important to deer because it helps them in their selection of food. It is hard to determine how much of what a deer eats is dependent upon taste instead of smell. Our taste buds can only differentiate between sweet, sour, salty, or bitter, but what we so often perceive as taste is really identified and qualified by our sense of smell. There is no evidence to prove that deer's sense of taste is any better than a human's.

Research has listed more than 650 species of plants in the northeastern United States that deer will eat. The list of what a deer won't eat would be extremely short, but what deer will eat varies from region to region. I am sure that what deer will eat is first recognized by smell, then confirmed by taste. I have watched three- to four-week-old fawns, starting to eat their first vegetation, select what their mothers ate in imitation. I have also seen fawns actually taste plants hanging from their mothers' mouths and thus became introduced to the proper vegetation.

Although it seems as if deer will eat almost anything, there are plants they will not eat because they do not like the taste. (Leonard Lee Rue III)

I was amazed one time to read that deer readily ate the pungent spice bush (*Lindera benzoin*) in Massachusetts because I have found that they won't touch it in my home area of northwestern New Jersey. Deer seem to have the innate knowledge of what plant compounds will be detrimental to the microflora and microfauna in their rumens. Plants such as spice bush contain volatile oils that inhibit the bacterial action needed for digestion, and, because of that, they are avoided. The deer in Massachusetts may have eaten the spice bush because no other browse was available. Daffodils also have a strong odor and are not eaten by deer. Plants of lavender will help to minimize deer damage in gardens as deer can't stand the smell or taste of it.

TOUCH

Touch is extremely important to deer because it is the thread that holds much of the fabric of their social life together.

The moment that a fawn is born, its mother commences to wash it clean. This cleaning is the start of the bonding process that imprints the fawn on the doe and vice versa. The doe washes the amniotic fluid and blood from the fawn to clean it and protect it from detection by predators. In the process, she is smelling and tasting the individual odor of her fawn, by which means she will be able to distinguish it from all others. She is also putting her individual odor, from her saliva, on the fawn, which will help the fawn to be able to imprint on her. The stimulation of touch is an important part of this procedure and is properly known as social grooming.

If the grooming is reciprocal, it is known as mutual grooming and is engaged in by deer of all sexes throughout their lives. In fraternal groups of bucks, social grooming is an acknowledgment of status because, although all members will engage in it, it is usually initiated by the lower bucks in the hierarchy. It may also serve the practical purpose of removing ticks from the

Bucks in fraternal groups frequently groom each other around the head and neck, removing ticks from each other that they cannot reach themselves. (Leonard Lee Rue III)

Deer stamp their feet out of nervousness and to send a warning to other deer. (Len Rue, Jr.)

head area where the deer can't reach itself.

Sexual stimulation is greatly increased by the tactile sensations employed by the adult bucks. Although the buck and doe may mutually groom each other's heads, both sexes rub against each other and each may lick the other's genital area. The latter is engaged in by does on occasion, but the practice by bucks is common and frequent. That is, it is common and frequently done by adult bucks, but seldom by yearling and two-and-one-half-year bucks. They just haven't lived long enough to gain the experience needed to be "good lovers." Expertise only comes with age.

At the first indication of potential danger—and any sound or odor not identified is a potential danger—deer stamp their feet. The vibrations travel through the ground, alerting all other deer in the area. Other deer facing the other direction may not see the flaring of the tail and rump hair, but will both hear and feel the stamping of the feet.

A Sixth Sense?

A sixth sense?

I would be remiss if I did not acknowledge that I have long believed that most wild creatures, deer included, have a sixth sense. Because psychic phenomena is hard to prove, many deer researchers don't even acknowledge the possibility of it occurring. I am pleased to say that is changing. The psychic sense is latent in all of us, although most of us live an existence removed from most dangers. But how often have you felt the hair raise on the back of your neck when you have not seen, heard, or smelled anything to cause that sensation? You just "felt" danger without actually feeling anything. All too often I have seen wildlife become intensely alert when they had not seen, heard, or smelled anything tangible; they just felt it. Almost everyone who has a pet has experienced the pet knowing what they, their owner, was going to do, or was thinking of doing, before they did anything.

Above: *Does constantly groom their fawns, reinforcing the bond between them. (Leonard Lee Rue III)*

Facing page: *An extremely alert whitetail buck focusing all of his senses on me. (Leonard Lee Rue III)*

Chapter Three

THE GLANDS

DEER LIVE IN A WORLD OF SCENT, THEIR OLFACTORY SENSES BEING THE MOST IMPORTANT OF all their senses. Deer constantly monitor the odor of everything in their environment. Scent is also their main means of communicating with other deer, which they do through urine, feces, and the secretions of their external glands.

White-tailed deer are forest creatures, living in the woods, along the edge of the woods, or in brushland. If you don't have high, woody cover (and standing cornfields are synonymous with high, woody cover), you don't have whitetails; it's just that simple. Because deer spend the bulk of their time in cover, visual communication is minimized.

Deer are social creatures that do not gather in large aggregations unless they are forced to do so when seeking nutritious food or winter cover. Deer usually travel in small familial or fraternal groups most of the year, and bucks usually travel alone during the rutting season; therefore, audible communication is also minimal.

With their visual and audible communication limited, their use of chemical signposts is paramount to deer's communication with one another. In all communication, one participant is the sender and the other, or others, are the receivers. The more information that can be sent at one time, the more the intent of the conveyor can be ascertained. The advantage of olfactory chemical communication is that the sender and receiver don't ever have to have physical contact with each other. Also, whereas audible communication is instantaneous, it is lost in the same fraction of time. Visual communication is also instantaneous, but only occasionally are long-lasting signals given. Chemical olfactory communication can be nearly instantaneous if the sender and receiver meet, but deposited scent continues to send messages for hours, days, and even weeks, depending on temperatures and atmospheric conditions.

Whitetail bucks frequently lick the scent from each other's forehead glands, and no one knows why they do it. (Len Rue, Jr.)

The deer's external glands, in order of importance, are its tarsal, forehead, preorbital, nasal, salivary, preputial, interdigital, and metatarsal, and there may be others that we are not aware of as yet.

THE TARSAL GLANDS

I rank the deer's tarsal (hock) glands as being the most important because the deer do. Bucks and does both have them, and both sexes engage in rub-urination. Fawns actively start using the glands when they are one to two weeks old, but I can't for the life of me tell you what message the fawns are trying to send.

The tarsal glands have subcutaneous sebaceous glands that exude an oily secretion through the skin via ducts alongside of the hair follicle. Erector pili muscles along the side of the hair sheath allow the hairs to be contracted so that they are tightly closed and resemble the bristles on a brush used to apply shoe polish. The closed hair minimizes the odor given off by this gland. When the deer is alarmed or aggressive, the erector pili muscles cause the tarsal hairs to be widely flared like a rosette, maximizing the scent dispersal because more surface area is exposed.

The pheromones given off by the glands themselves have been tested by Dietland Muller-Schwarze using chromatograms, and he found that, like its DNA, the secretions are unique to each animal, containing information about the animal's sex, age, and dominance. By extrapolation, that means that any of an individual deer's secretions would also be unique, and that is why the olfactory sense is the most important sense to deer.

Ordinarily, white-tailed deer urinate by simply spreading their hind legs and stooping slightly. When engaging in rub-urination, the deer balance themselves on their front legs, bring their hind legs together, then rub their tarsal glands against each other as the urine trickles down over the long hairs. Although the tarsal glands give off pheromones of their own, the dominant odor is caused by bacterial action on the residue of the urine trapped in the hairs.

Whitetails of both sexes engage in rub-urination throughout the year, but both sexes do it much more

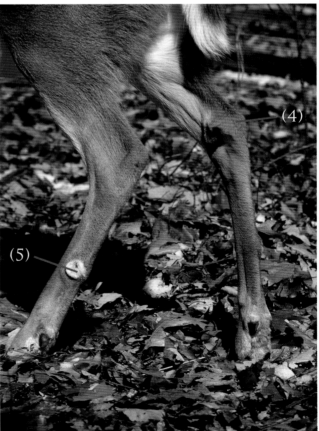

Right, top: *The forehead (1), preorbital (2), and nasal glands (3). (Leonard Lee Rue III)*

Right, bottom: *The tarsal (4) and metatarsal glands (5). (Leonard Lee Rue III)*

frequently during the rutting season. Triggered by testosterone, bucks rub-urinate during the rut, and the more dominant the buck, the more frequently he does it, and the darker the hair tufts are stained. I have seen dominant bucks whose tarsal hairs were black, as were all of the hairs on the inside of the foot from the gland down to the hoof.

The bucks will frequently lick the urine off their own tarsal glands. Lesser bucks in a fraternal group will also lick the urine off the dominant buck's tarsal gland. When two strange dogs meet, they check each other out by smelling the scent in the other's anal gland. When two strange bucks check each other out, they do it by sniffing each other's tarsal glands.

It is the combined odor of the pheromones and the urine on the tarsal glands that give dominant bucks their strong odor during the rutting season. Under good scenting conditions, I can smell a buck at a distance of two hundred to three hundred feet, even after he's gone.

There is absolutely no truth to the old hunters' dictum that says the tarsal gland has to be removed as soon as the buck is killed to prevent the gland from "tainting" the meat. I have always said that if the gland didn't taint the meat while the buck was alive—and it doesn't—it could not taint the meat when the deer was dead. However, I always remove the gland by cutting off the leg above the hock gland before I skin my deer. This prevents an accidental touching of the gland and the possible transferal of the scent to the meat by the hunter's hand. Tarsal glands that have been cut off and just air-dried make very good attractants when used while hunting; just hang them around your stand. They can be kept over the winter by placing them in an air-proof plastic bag and freezing them.

As a means of self-promotion and advertisement,

All white-tailed deer urinate on their tarsal glands throughout the year, but they do it more frequently during the rutting season. (Leonard Lee Rue III)

Above: *Depositing forehead scent on a "buck rub" is one of the whitetail's main means of communication. (Len Rue, Jr.)*

Facing page, both photos: *Many times a whitetail buck deposits scent from his forehead glands on a rub, then smells and often licks it off. (Len Rue, Jr.)*

elk urinate on the long hairs under their neck. Both elk and moose urinate in mud wallows and then roll in the goo, coating themselves with the urine-stained mud. White-tailed, mule, and blacktail deer urinate on their tarsal glands for the same purpose.

THE FOREHEAD GLANDS

In late October 1972, I photographed a white-tailed buck rubbing its forehead, not its antlers, on a stiff dead weed stalk, but at the time I did not know the significance of what I was seeing. Later on that same day, I saw the buck rub the bark off several small saplings with his rough antler bases, then rub his forehead, between the antlers, on the rubbed area.

I was sure he was depositing scent. I had watched dogs drag their anal glands on the ground, male gray squirrels drag their scrotums on tree limbs, and woodchucks and cats rub their mouths and cheek glands on objects, and I knew they were depositing scent. I was

sure the buck was, too, but I couldn't prove it.

It was not until the conclusive study on forehead glands, done by Thomas Atkeson and Larry Marchinton in 1992, that I had my proof. Atkeson and Marchinton studied white-tailed deer, both bucks and does, and discovered suderiferous glands in the skin. Their extended study showed that both bucks and does had the glands, but that bucks had many more of them. They also discovered that, although the glands were basically quiescent during most of the year, they become greatly enlarged during the rutting season with a great increase in secretions. I have seen bucks rub their forehead scent glands at all times of the year, but they do it gently, except in the rutting season.

It is now a well-known fact that the more dominant the buck, the more frequently he rubs and the darker his forehead becomes. The secretions not only darken the forehead but also, in extreme cases, the entire upper part of the face down the bridge of the

Whitetail bucks frequently rub the forehead glands, located behind the antlers and in front of the ears, on sticks. (Leonard Lee Rue III)

nose and the cheeks. To withstand the tremendous rubbing pressure that the bucks apply to this area, the skin is about one-quarter of an inch thick. It has always puzzled me that, despite the tremendous amount of rubbing the dominant bucks do, I have never seen one with all of the hairs rubbed off so that the bare skin could be seen.

I have discovered that if a buck is rubbing a four- to six-inch tree, he usually rubs with his forehead, directly between his antlers, as it is the only spot he can reach. If he rubs a sapling of about one inch in diameter, he prefers to rub the area behind his antlers, in front of his ears, alternating one side and then the other. This area apparently is the most richly endowed with glands.

Although does also have these forehead scent glands, I have only seen two does rub their foreheads against a sapling, and they did so with very little effort and pressure. However, the does are very interested in the rubs made by the dominant bucks, and I have seen them both smell and lick buck rubs and licking sticks (upright sticks that the buck first deposits forehead scent on and then licks off).

THE PREORBITAL GLANDS

The deer's preorbital or lacrymal glands are the tear ducts located on the forward edge of its eyes. While some researchers dismiss the importance of this gland, the deer do not. I have seen too many deer rub this gland on too much vegetation not to believe that it is important in sending chemical signals.

After watching hundreds and hundreds of bucks

Bucks often chew on overhead branches, depositing saliva scent. (Len Rue, Jr.)

rub their forehead and preorbital glands against overhead branches, I have to conclude that it is a very pleasurable stimulation. That may sound anthropomorphic, but the deer close their eyes and look as if they are enjoying it.

THE NASAL GLANDS

Scent glands have been found in the posterior portion of the deer's nostrils. These glands may deposit scent in conjunction with the preorbital and forehead glands. I cannot recall ever seeing a deer rub just its nostrils on a sapling or bush.

THE SALIVARY GLANDS

Deer have an ammonia-based scent in their saliva, which they use to leave their scent marking. An overhead branch is an integral part of any major scrape. The deer chew on the tip of the branch, crushing its tip with their premolars. They are not trying to eat

the tip—they are just greatly increasing the amount of crushed fiber ends. This causes the tip to have a rough surface area and allows it to hold a much greater quantity of saliva scent.

Most bucks drool drops, and even long strings, of saliva during the rutting season. The more dominant the buck, the more copiously he drools. As all animals are individuals and vary in what they do, different bucks drool different amounts. I have videotaped some dominant bucks drooling long strings of saliva constantly. Using an eye dropper to simulate the amount of drooling that I documented, I've concluded that it's safe to say some bucks drool more than a pint of saliva a day, painting their home range with their individual odor.

THE PREPUTIAL GLAND

The preputial gland, located at the tip of the buck's penis sheath, may add additional pheromones to the buck's urine as he urinates. I personally have not seen where the secretions of this gland play anything but a secondary role in scent making.

THE INTERDIGITAL GLAND

I recently discovered that the interdigital gland plays a far more important role in communication among deer than I ever before gave it credit. In November 1997, I spent from dawn to dusk watching a big dominant buck tending a doe that was in estrus. As deer usually breed only once every four hours, the time in between is spent resting, feeding a little, and, in the case of the buck, keeping younger bucks away from his doe. In the quiet interim, I constantly asked myself, "What can I learn that's new?"

The buck was tending the doe on a small area of dry, higher ground, surrounded by a muddy, boggy swamp. After hours of fruitless studying and pondering, I suddenly became aware that each time a young buck crossed the boggy area, or the big buck crossed the bog to chase the young one away, they both would stop and lick the mud from between their hooves on all four feet.

The interdigital glands are located between the deer's two center toes. The gland may be overlooked because the entrance to it is hidden by long, stiff hairs. If you run a cotton swab up in the gland about one and one-half to two inches, it will come out coated with a grayish secretion that has the consistency and odor of the wax that we have in our ears. This wax

A buck smelling an overhead branch on which scent has been deposited. (Leonard Lee Rue III)

coats the long hairs between the toes and oozes down between the hooves, thus leaving traces on the vegetation that the deer passes through or on the ground on which it walks. It is the scent that the deer follow when they are tracking one another.

In the ten days to two weeks following its birth, a fawn stays hidden while its mother stays away from it. From time to time, the fawn will get up and move anywhere from a few feet to a hundred feet or more. When the doe comes back to nurse her fawn, she knows the general area in which she left it, but she does not know precisely where it is. She tracks the fawn to its new bedding spot by following the scent of the interdigital gland.

Deer have a fantastic sense of smell, but I believe that of tracking dogs is far superior. A good dog can follow the scent of what it is following by picking up the scent from the nearby vegetation. Deer apparently can't do that; a buck follows the tracks of a doe by following her exact footsteps. Most hunters have seen bucks tracking does in the rutting season. The buck walks or trots along, his nose to the ground, his tail raised high, and he usually gives off a soft grunt every few seconds, as he follows the scent of the doe's interdigital gland.

The buck uses scent from eight glands in making a scrape. He usually hooks the overhead branch with his antlers and then chews on the tips. He then rubs the branch over his forehead, preorbital, and possibly his nasal glands. Pawing the ground vigorously, he liberally coats the dirt with his interdigital scent from between his splayed hooves. Next he stands in the middle of the scrape and rub-urinates. In the process, the buck has signed the scrape with his own individual signature. (See chapter 4 for more information on scrapes.)

At times, the interdigital scent is used to shout a silent warning. When deer are alarmed, they stamp their feet repeatedly, putting extra interdigital scent on the ground. Other deer passing that spot later will be alerted to the possibility of danger.

Above: *This buck is tracking a doe by the scent left by her interdigital glands. (Len Rue, Jr.)*

Left: *The interdigital gland is located between the deer's two center toes, about two inches above the hooves. (Leonard Lee Rue III)*

All photos: *A buck on a scrape first chews on the overhead branches, depositing saliva, and then rubs forehead scent on them. Next he paws the scrape alternately with his front feet. Lastly he steps into the scrape and rub-urinates there. (Leonard Lee Rue III)*

Bucks chase does so consistently during the rutting season that they become exhausted. If the weather is warm, they will pant like a dog to cool off. I also believe they will sweat-wet. (Len Rue, Jr.)

THE METATARSAL GLAND

On the outside of a whitetail's hind foot, about midway between the heel and the hoof tips, is the metatarsal gland. It is a gland that is about one inch long on the whitetail, three inches long on the blacktail, and five inches long on a mule deer. In the center of the hair tuft is a very dark gray, dry, cornified ridge.

It is very difficult to accurately describe an uncommon odor. We usually try to do so by comparing it to something with which we are more familiar. Some researchers claim that the metatarsal gland gives off a garlicky odor. The ring of skin surrounding the gland does have both sebaceous and sudoriferous glands, but I have never been able to detect any moisture or odor from this gland. I believe that the metatarsals are glands that are atrophying and which, in time, like the human appendix, will disappear through disuse.

WHAT ABOUT SWEAT GLANDS?

Most researchers claim that deer do not have sweat glands. It is a well-known fact that when deer are stressed or have exerted themselves, they pant visibly through the open mouth like a dog. The rapid exchange of air helps to dispel body heat via the lungs.

Human sweat has no odor. The odor that we associate with sweat is due to bacterial action on the sweat. If deer do have sweat glands, their sweat would probably also be odorless. I have always believed that deer do have sweat glands, because so often during the rutting season I have seen bucks with their body and neck hair so wet that the hair parts in segments. I realize that the deer do not sweat-lather like horses do, but they do get wet. The question of whether or not deer sweat needs additional study.

Chapter Four

COMMUNICATION

FOR MANY YEARS, IN MY BOOKS AND LECTURES, I HAVE SAID THAT WE WILL NOT TRULY understand deer until we understand their communication. The greatest strides in deer research over the last few years have been in the field of communication, and because of this we now know more about deer than ever before.

The deer's entire social life is governed by dominance. Dominance is basically determined by size, strength, and hormones. Fawns usually start to assert dominance when they are three to four weeks old. Fawns of dominant does usually become dominant themselves because they are usually born sooner in the season, have better birth weight, and have access to more milk and better vegetation because of their mothers' status. Like rich kids, they just get a head start in life that they are usually able to maintain throughout their lives. Dominance is not a constant condition; it is, instead, in a constant state of flux and, as such, extracts a high toll on the dominant animal. Dominant animals must always be willing and able to fight for their dominance, but only if they have to. That's why they communicate.

VOCALIZATIONS AND AURAL COMMUNICATION

Deer are not very vocal creatures, although they do have a wider repertoire of sounds than most folks are aware. Many people now know that deer grunt because bowhunters use grunt tubes as standard hunting equipment. Native Americans used both grunt and bleat calls for hunting deer.

Deer often flare the hairs of their tail when they are nervous or alarmed. The flared tail tells other deer to be alert for possible danger in the area. (Leonard Lee Rue III)

Big bucks grunt when they are tracking a doe, warning off a rival, or before and during combat. The bigger the buck, the deeper the grunt, because both the pitch and the volume depend upon the deer's chest size. Hunters should not use their grunt tubes at the lowest pitch possible because the extremely low note may scare away even a good-sized buck.

A does also grunts softly when she returns to the area in which she has hidden her fawn. Upon hearing its mother's grunt, the fawn leaps from where it has been hiding and usually responds with a mewing call. While nursing, the fawn makes an eager whining sound that can be heard above the sound of its suckling. If lost or frightened, the fawn gives out with a very loud bleating call. The bleat is both shrill and strident and carries for a considerable distance. Because a doe cannot recognize her own fawn by its voice, several does may respond to the fawn's cry for help.

The best known sound of the whitetail is the snort because it is louder than any of the others. People hear this explosive sound most often because deer often use it in response to the presence of humans.

There are two different snorts that vary in intensity and purpose. The regular snort is given by the deer with their mouths closed; they expel air forcefully from the diaphragm through the nasal passageways, causing the closed nostrils to flutter. Deer snort this way when they are surprised or startled. It puts every deer on full alert, but they usually try to discover what it was that surprised or startled them before they turn to flee. This snort is frequently accompanied by foot stamping. The stamping is both heard and felt. Both the snort and the stamping may be given a number of times.

The second snort is now being called the snort-wheeze. This sound is blasted out of both the deer's nose and partially opened mouth, and it is produced by both the compression of air and use of the larynx. It has a much longer, higher pitched sound than the regular snort and, when given, causes all deer to explode into action. There is no hesitation, there is no trying to locate or identify the danger, there is no pattern to the deer's dispersal; they are gone, every last one of them.

Although it is not done by one deer to attract another, rattling antlers together is a common device now used by hunters to attract deer, and attract deer it does. Many bucks simply cannot resist the sound of antlers crashing together because it is the sound bucks make while fighting. Young bucks want to see the "big guys" battling it out, mature bucks want to see who the competition is, and all bucks want to see if any estrus doe is there waiting on the sidelines.

BODY LANGUAGE

As a student of body language, I find it interesting to see if what people are saying with their mouths agrees with what their bodies say they really mean. All deer are students of body language; it is a basic necessity for maintaining order in their lives.

The white-tailed deer is so named because the under surface of its tail is white, while the upper surface is brown or may be partly or all black. When the deer is alarmed, the tail may be raised and the hair flared out, giving the tail a width of eleven inches or more in big deer. Usually the erector pili muscles reverse the rump hair so that the entire deer is white when viewed from the rear. This is a danger signal to every deer that sees it, putting them on instant alert.

A doe that has fawns usually dashes off, allowing her tail to flop loosely from side to side. This bouncing white tail is a beacon for the fawns to follow on even the darkest of nights.

Many bucks will run off with their tails held high, but just as many run off with their tails clamped down. A deer that doesn't want to be seen turns its rump hair inward and clamps its tail down so that no white is visible.

The "hard stare" is the most frequently seen body language used by both the dominant does and bucks. With does, the head is usually held high, and the ears are laid almost straight back or slightly downward and back. The dominant doe will then walk directly towards her adversary. If the adversary does not give way and move off, the dominant doe will probably deliver a forward kick with one of her front feet. If the adversary presents a challenge, the dominant doe will rise up on her hind legs and flail out with her front feet. Often both deer will rise up and strike out, and the outcome is then determined by strength. After the clash, the winner usually just needs to give the hard stare to maintain dominance.

Bucks also use the hard stare to intimidate rivals, but they approach each other in a circular, sidling fashion. Their ears will be laid back, but the head is held lower than the body, and the chin is tucked in so that the antlers are projected forward. Their erector pili muscles will have all of the deer's body hair standing

Two bucks dash off with their tails clamped down while the third has his tail raised and flared. (Leonard Lee Rue III)

Does assert dominance by fighting—standing erect and striking out with their forefeet. (Len Rue, Jr.)

Above: *Bucks sometimes show aggression by pawing the ground with their forefeet. (Leonard Lee Rue III)*

Right: *This buck is displaying extreme aggression. His chin is tucked in so that his antlers project forward, all of his body hair is erected to make him appear larger, his ears are laid back, and he is walking with a stiff-legged gait in a sidling manner. This posture is called the "hard stare." (Leonard Lee Rue III)*

on end, which increases the bucks' apparent body size and also causes them to turn a much darker color because now the depth of the hair is visible instead of just the flat surface. The bucks approach each other in a stiff-legged gait; they will probably be grunting and occasionally even make a high-pitched whine. Their tarsal glands will be widely flared, giving off scent.

Only equal animals fight. Usually just the hard stare approach is enough to put any lesser buck to flight. It is important to remember that the buck sends the message that he hopes will establish his dominance, but which will allow him to conserve energy by not having to fight to prove it. Every deer knows exactly how big he is in body and antler size compared to ev-

ery other buck he meets. In the wild, might makes right; that innate knowledge is reinforced by visual communication.

During the period when the bucks have no antlers, or when their antlers are soft and growing, they fight like the does, by standing erect and flailing with their forefeet. The deer's hard, sharp hooves can be dangerous weapons, although they are used as clubs, not knives.

RUBS, SCRAPES, AND OTHER SCENT COMMUNICATION

In countries where many people do not have radios, televisions, or newspapers, information is posted on the walls for everyone to see. The person who puts up

Above: *Only big bucks rub big trees. (Len Rue, Jr.)*

Left: *Note that bucks do most of their rubbing with their antler bases, not with their tines, because the roughness of the pearlation and the burr actually grates the bark off. (Leonard Lee Rue III)*

the poster, the sender, does not know who will read it, but the message is loud and clear for all who pass that way. And that's what deer do with their chemical signposts. (Although all deer behavior is essentially the same over the entire continent, the timing of the chemical communication outlined in this section is basic for the northern two-thirds of North America.)

The bucks make their first rubs to remove the drying, itching velvet from their antlers. The mature bucks' antlers harden and are peeled free from velvet usually one to two weeks sooner than the younger bucks' antlers. They also make rubs two to three weeks sooner than younger bucks and make scrapes at least one month sooner.

Very little rubbing is done by the bucks during Sep-

tember and the first week of October. All deer go through a period of mandatory lipogenesis; in other words, they must build layers of fat if they are to survive the coming winter. Bucks start to fatten in July as antler development is completed. Does start to fatten later, after they have weaned their fawns. The last two weeks of September and the first week in October will see most of the acorns, the deer's most favored food, fall from the trees. Acorns are rich in carbohydrates, easily gathered when there is a good crop, and readily assimilated. The deer will grow fat faster on acorns than on any other food. The fall of 1998 was a great year for acorns in the northeastern United States, with more than five hundred pounds of acorns to the acre in the oak forests.

Above: *Notice the bark embedded between the pearlation on this buck's antlers; it is there because he rubbed on saplings. (Len Rue, Jr.)*

Facing page, both photos: *I was the first to record deer using a licking stick. This licking stick is a sapling about one inch in diameter and broken off about thirty-six inches above the ground. The deer rubbed scent on it and then licked it off. Such a stick is a magnet to all deer. (Leonard Lee Rue III)*

Old timers believed that bucks only made one rub, when they removed the velvet from their antlers, and that every rub denoted another buck. Today we know that most bucks make hundreds and hundreds of rubs each season. I have watched a single buck make dozens of rubs per day.

Rub making starts in mid-September and increases between the first and second week in October, just as the rutting season gets started.

(The rutting season, by my definition, consists of the length of time that a mature buck's neck is swollen, and this is generally from October 15 to December 15. It coincides with the maximum production of the hormone testosterone by the bucks' testes. Bucks are capable of breeding before their necks start to swell and can continue after the swelling has gone down but for northern bucks the rut is basically over by December 15.)

Most rubs are made on saplings between one to two inches in diameter. Rubbing serves many purposes, and the closer it becomes to the peak of the breeding season, the larger are the rubs the bucks make.

The bucks prefer saplings of that size because they are resilient and push back when the buck pushes against them, making it an isometric exercise. Big bucks also rub saplings, but only big bucks rub big trees. I have seen trees twelve inches in diameter scarred by big bucks, and trees up to eight inches shredded. The exercise that the buck gets from rubbing hardens the muscle mass of the neck that has been built up by the testosterone. It is a physical conditioning for the fights that will follow.

In rubbing, the buck actually grates the bark from the sapling, using the pearlation, the rough ridges on the main antler beam and the burr at the antler base. Tremendous pressure is applied in both the upward and downward thrusts. As the buck scrapes the inner bark loose, he usually pauses long enough to eat the strips. After the bark has been peeled, the buck also rubs his forehead scent gland liberally over the sapling. When finished, the white wood of the rub is a visual sign that can be seen for a long distance. The rub is also an olfactory sign from the deposition of both the forehead and salivary scent.

Timing Is Everything

To understand the exact timing of the deer's yearly cycle, it must be remembered that the white-tailed deer is an animal that evolved in the warmer climes and has been working its way north ever since. In Central America, the whitetails are not on an annual cycle. They can and do breed in every month of the year. In the Deep South, below the thirty-second degree latitude, the rutting season is usually quite long, with the peak of the breeding taking place in December and January. I have seen bucks still in velvet the first week in December in Alabama and have photographed peak breeding activity in the first week in January in Louisiana and Texas. Their window of opportunity is longer because it is not as critical for the fawns to be born at a precise time as it is in the north.

For the upper two-thirds of the United States and southern Canada, the bulk of the breeding takes place between November 7 and 12, with some does being bred a little earlier and some a little later. John J. Ozoga's research has consistently shown November 16 through 18 to be the peak of the rut in northern Michigan. The so-called "second rut" occurs around December 5. In this period, does that did not conceive during the primary rut, and some of the doe fawns, will be bred. Northern deer have a very narrow window of opportunity because, in order for the fawns to survive, it is imperative for them to be born between mid-May and mid-June, when the most nutritious vegetation is at is productive peak and the weather is not an adverse factor.

Although the mature bucks usually peel the velvet from their antlers the first week in September, some may peel as early as August 25. Even younger bucks will usually be peeled by September 7. The velvet may be rubbed off in as little as half an hour, or some strips may hang on for days. Dominance among the bucks shifts almost hourly, according to which one peels first.

My friend Joe Taylor had a spike buck in his herd peel two days before the mature bucks. This is most unusual, but it can happen. For those two days, the spike buck lorded it over the big bucks and ran them ragged, jabbing them with his spikes at every opportunity. Both mature bucks peeled the same night and promptly killed the spike buck.

Deer deposit scent on almost every overhead branch they can reach. Most of these "signposts" go undetected by humans because there is no corresponding scrape underneath. (Len Rue, Jr.)

Whereas buck rubs are most common along the edge of the woodland, because more young saplings grow on the edge, I have found most licking sticks in the forest itself. These lesser known signposts are not left along trails but seem to be made as the bucks wander through the forest gathering acorns.

Licking sticks are usually thirty to forty inches high, and, although the tops have been broken off by rubbing, the sticks are not so dry yet as to lose their resiliency. They are usually one-half to one inch in diameter and can be recognized because the top eight to ten inches will be entirely devoid of bark. Because this is the only visible sign, they are usually overlooked by most hunters—but not by the deer. Licking sticks draw deer like iron filings to a magnet.

Almost all of the rubbing done by the bucks will be done by the area of the forehead behind the ears and in front of the antlers. The deer will rub for perhaps thirty seconds, then lick off the scent deposited. It will rub again and lick it off, continuing this activity for a period of five minutes or more. Although I have never seen a doe rub the stick, I have seen them smell and lick it.

The least known but most common chemical signpost is the rubbing of the forehead scent gland by bucks on overhead branches. During World War II, signs saying "Kilroy was here" were chalked and painted on everything, all over the world, by U.S. servicemen and -women. I haven't the foggiest notion of who Kilroy was, but the signs were ubiquitous and so is the overhead signing by deer. I don't believe there is a protruding branch anywhere that has not been rubbed on by deer; they do it year round. Some bucks stand upright on their hind legs to reach high overhead branches. These signs remain mainly unseen by humans because there is nothing to see if you don't witness the deer actually doing it, as I have on thousands of occasions. Rubbing on overhead branches leaves only a chemical signal.

It is at the start of the rutting season that the mature bucks construct their major advertising billboards that we call scrapes. With just two exceptions, every primary deer scrape that I have ever seen was created

Right, both photos: *Major scrapes are almost always under an overhead branch that has been broken off and chewed upon by the deer. (Leonard Lee Rue III)*

Signposts and the Social System

Research has shown that in a socially balanced deer herd where mature bucks, two-and-one-half-year olds, yearlings, and fawn bucks all are present, the mature bucks' chemical signposts cause the lesser bucks to produce corticoids. These corticoids inhibit testicular growth and function, thus reducing the production of testosterone, which reduces the social stress of competition. If this leavening effect is destroyed by the removal of all of the mature bucks by hunters, the deer's social system breaks down, and the breeding season becomes more chaotic. This chaos, in turn, takes a tremendous caloric toll on all of the deer. Although the younger bucks are perfectly capable of breeding all the does, their inexperience causes much more chasing, fighting, and stress throughout the entire herd. These extra efforts will cause all of the deer to go into the winter in poorer condition, which may result in higher mortality. Henry Jacobson believes that this stress of early breeding also will prevent young bucks from ever realizing their full potential size.

This breakdown of a normal social system and resulting chaotic breeding frenzy does not happen to just white-tailed deer. It is a common occurrence with most Cervidae and with many predators. Among wolves and coyotes, for example, only the Alpha male and female breed, limiting the pack's size. The removal of the Alpha pair allows all of the other members of the pack to breed, producing an explosion in the population. The deer's social system works just a little differently. Although all of the does will be bred, the dominant buck will do the bulk of the chasing, fighting, and breeding. This allows the suppressed, younger males to go into the winter in much better shape, increasing their chances of survival and thus ensuring them a chance for dominance in the future.

under an overhanging branch. The overhead branch is first hooked with the antlers, then chewed upon by the mouth and rubbed over the forehead, preorbital, and nasal glands. The buck paws the earth beneath the branch, sometimes throwing clods of dirt fifteen to twenty feet. Over time the pawing will create a saucerlike depression, with the average scrape being approximately thirty inches in diameter, although some may be smaller and others much larger. After pawing the earth, the buck steps into the scrape and rub-urinates in the center. Other deer will be attracted to the scrape by the various chemical signals left by the buck, and they will also be attracted to the smell of fresh earth.

The scent-soaked scrape serves many purposes. The primary scrapes are usually made by the dominant males. They are a threat and a challenge to other dominant bucks; they are an advertisement and attractant to all the does; and they serve to intimidate and suppress the libido of younger bucks. The scrapes will be scraped again by other dominant males that pass that way, as they add their own scented signature. Just as dogs urinate on top of other dogs' urine, so mature bucks scrape their scent messages on top of those of other mature bucks. Yearling bucks will visit the scrapes, but they usually do not rub-urinate or scrape. I have seen lesser bucks that were accompanying a dominant buck check out the scrape but not urinate in it, undoubtedly intimidated by the odor of all the mature bucks. I have also, on two occasions, seen does smell and urinate in a scrape, but they did no scraping.

Some scrapes become traditional and are used by successive generations of bucks over the years. Some scrapes are used just once. Many scrapes will be cleaned and re-used by the most dominant buck each time he passes. Because the most dominant buck expands his range two to three times during the rutting season, he may not pass the scrape but once a week. Primary scrapes are good focal spots for hunters to concentrate their efforts, but even though more bucks travel in the daytime during the rut, mature, dominant males may travel only at night due to hunting pressure, and the hunter may never see the buck at his scrape.

PART II

The Deer's Year

A sight to gladden any hunter's heart: the beautiful October foliage and a magnificent whitetail buck. (Len Rue, Jr.)

JANUARY

January is a time of great hardship for the deer in the north. Most are held captive, in the deer yards they entered so readily in December, by deep snow, severe cold, and biting winds.

Deer yards offer many advantages because they are microclimates unto themselves. An ideal deer yard is usually in a low swampy area that has a good stand of white cedar trees, a very nutritious winter deer food. However, most yards are less than ideal because they are severely overbrowsed. In my area of northwestern New Jersey, the deer seldom have to yard up, but when they do, it is in thickets of red cedar or rhododendron swamps.

The most important feature of any yard is vegetation thick enough to break the force of the wind. Large deer in good condition can withstand all the cold in the world; they can't stand to be exposed to strong wind, which blows the cold through their hair, causing heat loss due to convection. Thick vegetation can reduce the force of the wind from twenty to five miles per hour, which, at zero degrees Fahrenheit ambient temperature, is the difference between zero degrees and minus thirty-one degrees Fahrenheit.

It also should be instantly apparent to anyone who has ever looked that the snow is always melted away from tree trunks as the trees give off heat and absorb and reflect the weak sun's rays. This tree heat also raises the temperature in the area ever so slightly.

In addition to breaking the force of the wind, thick cover provides a canopy, which holds most of the snow aloft where much of the moisture will evaporate as it melts. Once snow gets up to eighteen to twenty inches deep, all deer have great difficulty traveling. Deeper snow causes them to bound, an action that is extremely expensive in caloric consumption, particularly when the deer are subsisting on inferior and greatly diminished food supplies. Less snow means the deer can travel with less effort and expend fewer calories.

Yarded deer soon build a network of trails throughout the yard, which greatly facilitates their ability to move about. However, because all of the deer use the same trails in their search for food, everything edible is soon consumed. Even with their lowered metabo-

Deer usually yard in evergreen cover when possible because the dense vegetation breaks the force of the wind. (Len Rue, Jr.)

Above: *This buck has just been disturbed from his bed in a winter wonderland. (Leonard Lee Rue III)*

Left: *When snow becomes more than eighteen inches deep, all deer must bound in order to travel. This is very exhausting for the deer and very caloric expensive. (Leonard Lee Rue III)*

Above: *It is a sign of a food shortage when deer eat twigs larger in diameter than a match stick. (Leonard Lee Rue III)*

Right: *That deer don't allow snow to cover and insulate themselves when they bed is evidence that they are a southern species steadily expanding their range northward. (Leonard Lee Rue III)*

lism, the deer still need about three pounds of nutritious vegetation per one hundred pounds of body weight per day. As the nutritious food is in short supply in most deer yards, the deer usually run a negative caloric balance. Even if the deer are able to obtain some food, it is usually of such low quality that they expend more energy in obtaining and processing it than they get in caloric intake. In many cases, the deer would be better off if they did not eat at all and just lived on the fat stored in their bodies.

The amount of fat stored within a deer's body can be likened to a bank savings passbook. Everything that the deer eats is entered as a deposit. Daily body maintenance (all bodily functions of heart, lungs, and liver such as respiration, digestion, and elimination), causes steady withdrawals from the account of about eight

hundred to twelve hundred calories a day, per deer, according to the deer's age and size. Resting, feeding, walking, trotting, running, and fighting all have different caloric expenditure rates, with a buck using up to six thousand calories a day during the rutting season. Winter is a time of almost constant caloric withdrawals. Unlike the U.S. government, the deer—and you and I—cannot spend more than we make; we go broke, the deer die.

Many mammals, including you and me, involuntarily shiver when we become cold. The shivering actually causes the body to produce more heat, but comes at the expense of more food consumption. Between their lowered metabolic rate and the very real lack of food, deer do not have the option of shivering. I have never seen deer shiver, even at temperatures of minus

thirty degrees Fahrenheit.

In the north, where the cold keeps the snow soft and fluffy, the depth of snow that keeps the deer in yards also serves to keep many predators out, particularly dogs. Where or when thawing and freezing occur, a crust soon forms. The crust will often support the large feet and weight of the predators, but not the smaller, sharp hooves of the deer. When the chased deer are able to stay on their network of trails, they can usually outrun the predators. Deer that are forced from the trails break through the crusted snow and soon fall victim to the predators. Deer that try to negotiate smooth ice are also at a distinct disadvantage because the hard rims of their hooves allow no traction. In falling, the deer frequently dislocate their legs and have to lie there until they die or are killed.

Anyone interested in deer should leave them alone in the winter. Don't travel into their yards to see how they are faring because the tracks made by snow machines, skis, or snowshoes compact the snow, giving predators an open highway directly into the deer's sanctuary.

In the winter, the deer are forced to eat browse almost exclusively because all other types of vegetation have died down or are buried beneath the snow. In the deer's yard, constant overbrowsing quickly removes all of the succulent browse, and deer are often forced to eat twigs up to the diameter of a wood pencil. To obtain these large twigs, the deer have to take them sideways in their mouth and cut them using their third premolars and first molars, top and bottom. Cutting and chewing such heavy fiber produces undue wear

Above, both photos: *Deer are strong swimmers and readily take to water to escape from their enemies. In the southern United States, where winter weather is mild, and lakes and rivers do not freeze, whitetails are able to use the water to elude their natural enemies all year long. (Len Rue, Jr.)*

on these eight teeth, a condition often exhibited in older deer.

The bark on larger twigs is usually three years old and has far less nutrition than the new sprouts that the deer eat in the spring. The larger twigs also have about eight times more fiber and lignin, most of which is indigestible in the deer's stomach. In the north, twigs also are likely to be frozen when eaten, and it takes a lot of calories just to thaw them for processing. I have found many deer dead of starvation with their stomachs full of large twigs, red cedar, and rhododendron leaves, foods with little nutritional value.

That deer did not originate in the north is borne out by the fact that they do not properly utilize snow as do caribou and moose. Both of these cervids always lie down into fresh snow beds, allowing the snow to envelop their bodies. By doing so, the snow acts as a blanket of insulation, helping to keep the animals warm. Deer don't do that. Deer may make beds in fresh snow, but they always paw a hole in the snow first. They then lie down in the hole, losing the blanket effect of enveloping snow. In deep snow, the hole does all but eliminate the effects of any wind, so it does provide some benefit. Many times I have watched big deer kick little deer out of their snow beds and then lie down in the same bed.

In the south, the deer usually have slightly smaller bodies and weigh considerably less then their northern counterparts because they do not have to store as much fat on their bodies. Except for the deer in the Appalachian Mountain chain, most southern deer are not exposed to extreme cold or deep snow. Dogs are not as much of a problem as they are in the north because the deer can usually find sufficient food all year long and are not winter stressed. When pursued by dogs, most southern deer escape by taking to water.

In the north, although some bucks lose their antlers in December, most bucks shed them in the month of January. The buck's testosterone level drops after the rut, about the middle of December. The more dominant buck usually loses his antlers first because exhaustion and stress take their toll on his body, and his testicles begin to shrink, thus lowering the production of testosterone. Constantly decreasing amounts of daylight in December also causes diminished pituitary gland activity, but this affects all bucks about equally.

When the testosterone level drops, a specialized layer of cells at the base of the antlers, called osteoclasts, begins to reabsorb the calcium from the antler. The solid antlers become porous at the base, forming narrow, sharply pointed spicules. Eventually, the weight of the antler causes it to snap off at the narrowest point of the spicules. You can easily feel the roughness at the breaking point on either the antler base or pedicle.

Younger bucks that have been prevented from breeding keep their antlers longer. Even big bucks that have been penned up so they haven't been able to breed keep their antlers longer. Captive bucks that do a lot of breeding but who are fed a nutritious diet will keep their antlers longer. Southern bucks that have access to sufficient natural food all through the winter keep their antlers longer. The mild winters of 1997–

Above, both photos: *Bucks seldom lose both of their antlers at the exact same time. (Len Rue, Jr.)*

1998 and 1998–1999 allowed many bucks to keep their antlers longer. Hundreds of my readers from all sections of the country have written me that they had seen bucks carrying antlers up to and even into the first part of May. The one thing we have learned is that many different factors determine the timing of the casting of a buck's antlers.

I have seen many instances of a buck losing both of his antlers in the same night, but only three times have I found a pair of antlers lying together, having been shed at precisely the same time. On two occurrences I saw running bucks make a jump and land hard enough to jar an antler loose. I once shot a buck whose antler fell off in my hand when I picked up his head by the antler to move him.

One of only three sets of antlers that I have ever found that were shed at the same time. (Len Rue, Jr.)

There is minimal bleeding when the antlers are cast, and this is caused by a slight tearing of the skin that surrounds the antler base below the burr. Arterial valves prevent excess bleeding at that point. I don't believe the bleeding consists of more than about twenty drops of blood. There probably is little or no pain due to a lack of nerve endings. The bleeding stops

I have always said that the deer are not inhabitants of mature forests because the canopy of mature forests blocks out all sunlight and keeps it from reaching the forest floor; without the necessary sunlight, plants cannot grow, so there is nothing for the deer to eat. The deer are "forest fringe" animals, living at the edge of the forest where they can feed upon emergent vegetation.

"Edge" is one of the most important features of habitat. Most edge occurs where the forest meets open areas that have been cut, burned, or farmed. It may also be a roadside or lakeshore area. Wherever the sunlight can get to the earth, it allows such a profusion of new brush to grow that, when it is leafed out, you will not be able to see through it. Unless you have too many deer. Too many deer destroy this edge, eating their favored foods, creating the browse lines—"high lines"—that allow us to look into the forest. It does not matter what the number of deer is; when you can stand in a field and look into a forest, you have too many deer.

The destruction of the edge reduces or eliminates the populations of song and game birds and small mammals that depend upon such cover for their own survival. It is not just the destruction of the rain forests in Central and South America that poses such a threat to our migratory songbirds' survival, it is also the elimination of the understory of our forests by deer.

Very little blood is shed when a buck's antler is cast, and a scab soon forms. (Leonard Lee Rue III)

almost instantly, and the pedicle changes from having a raw red appearance to a glazed surface to the start of a scab in a few hours. The scab falls off in twelve to fourteen days, revealing a puckered dry skin having short bristly hairs that stand on end. It is this skin that will be the start of the velvet covering when the new antlers start to grow.

FEBRUARY

February is the starvation month. If winter comes in November, with extreme cold and deep snow forcing the deer to yard up early, most will have used up their fat reserves by the middle of February. When that happens, the fawns die first because they have a smaller body size and fewer fat reserves. Larger deer can reach higher to feed upon the limited food available. Even the most caring does will drive their own fawns from food because when it comes down to actual survival, the doe's own life is more important to her, and to the herd, than the fawn's life.

Although the bucks are larger than the does and can reach even higher for available food, their chances of surviving are less than the does'. If winter arrived early, the mature bucks, having lost up to 20 to 25 percent of their body weight in the November rut, will have had no chance of recouping that loss. A severe, early winter will kill off almost all of the mature bucks, but the loss to the herd is not as draconian as it may appear. The loss of the mature bucks will mean fewer trophy deer for the hunter the next fall, but as the starvation usually takes place in February, the bucks' superior genes will have already been passed on to the next generation through the does that they bred the previous November.

There is more than an hour of additional daylight on a day in February than on the same date in January. The sun is still low on the horizon but angling higher each day. Winter still holds everything locked in its icy grip, but that grip is gradually being weakened. Hunting for deer is over in most of the states, and the deer are more relaxed. Very little activity takes place at night as yet. Their metabolism is still in the idle mode, and the deer are still inactive for at least 80 percent of their time. Except where the northern deer are yarded up, most deer will be feeding on south-facing slopes. The activity starts about 9 A.M. with bucks, does, and fawns tolerating each other as they take advantage of whatever warmth the sun provides. They usually feed for about an hour, then bed until

Because of their smaller body size and weight, starvation takes its greatest toll on last spring's fawns. (Leonard Lee Rue III)

In late winter, deer feed primarily during the daylight hours and, if not yarded, concentrate wherever food is available. (Leonard Lee Rue III)

about 11 A.M. when they move and feed again. At about noon, they bed again, rising at 3 P.M. to feed until about 4 P.M.

Absolutely nothing about wildlife is set in stone. What I am describing in this book will happen to most of the deer most of the time over most of the United States. But variables change circumstances.

MARCH

March finds a tremendous transition taking place in both the deer and their world. The vernal equinox takes place on or about March 20, the time of the year when the amount of daylight and darkness are exactly equal. However, it is not the equality of the number of

The El Nino Effect

The El Nino effect during the winter of 1997–1998 had more far-reaching results than most folks know. That winter was the warmest I have experienced in my seventy-three years. A recent report stated that residents of just the United States saved more than five billion dollars on fuel to heat their homes in the winter of 1997–1998. I don't know how many billions in calories the deer saved, but I know it saved millions of their lives. I wrote then that the summer of 1998 would see the largest fawn recruitment rate because of lowered mortality rates. I said that more fawns would be born, and they would have heavier birthing weights, be in better health, and get more sustenance from their dams because both the does and the vegetation would be in better shape because of the extremely moderate winter.

I wrote then that more trophy bucks would be taken in the fall hunting season of 1998 because more of the mature bucks would survive the moderate winter. All of the bucks would also come through the winter in much better shape because they had been able to move about far more and could get better food. The bucks would not have to spend all spring playing catch-up. As their bodies were in better shape to start with, the new vegetation that they ate in the spring could go directly to body growth and antler development. And this was true to some extent, no matter where the deer were nor how poor the habitat. Several taxidermists told me that they had gotten more big-antlered deer in than ever before. El Nino was a blessing to all deer.

Facing page: *An easy winter, like the one caused by El Nino in 1997–1998, lets the bucks come into spring in better shape and allows them to grow bigger-than-average antlers by fall. (Len Rue, Jr.)*

daylight hours that is most important, but the fact that since December 21 the amount of daylight in a twenty-four hour period has been steadily increasing at a little less than one and one-half minutes per day.

The increasing amount of daylight period is picked up by the retina of the deer's eye, which acts as a photoelectric cell, sending electrical impulses to the pineal gland. This gland is often referred to as a "third eye." The pineal gland is responsible for sending a chemical stimulus to the endocrine system that determines the timing of the behavior of most of the world's creatures. It is the pineal gland that sets the biological clock, triggering behaviors such as migration, hibernation, breeding seasons, and parturition.

In March, the deer's metabolism kicks back into high gear, which greatly increases the deer's desire and need for more food. Over most of the country, grasses sprout along spring runs and on sun-warmed hillsides. Buds swell with nutrition in anticipation. Briar bushes of all kinds—blackberry, raspberry, barberry—sprout early and fast and the twig tips are eagerly eaten by deer.

It is particularly important for the does to get all of the extra food possible, because with their increased metabolic rate comes a growth spurt in the fetuses they are carrying. It was long believed that does on a starvation diet would often abort or reabsorb fetuses that had died. The latest research has shown most fetuses are not lost during the hard months of winter but are carried to full term; undernourished fetuses are either born dead or so much underweight that they don't survive. It seems that the dividing line is a minimum of a five-pound birth weight. Underweight fawns are too weak to stand to be able to nurse. Fawns weighing less than five pounds usually die within three to four days. Fawns above that minimum birth weight have their chances of survival increased with each additional pound. Singletons usually weigh more than either one of a set of twins.

The metabolic increase also triggers a growth spurt in all of last year's fawns that made it through the winter. This growth is particularly noticeable in their faces. Fawns, when born, have shortened muzzles due to the fact that their jawbones have to accommodate only three premolars on each side of their top and bottom jaws. At four months of age, the jawbone lengthens to accommodate the first molar. At six months, the second molar erupts through the jawbone. At twelve to

Although deer have been recorded eating more than 650 different types of food, much of the food on that list will be eaten of necessity and not by choice. When deer overpopulate an area, they soon destroy all of their favored foods and are forced to eat whatever else is available.

Deer feed heavily upon nutritious forbs in spring and summer, but they do so because there is usually not enough available browse. Overpopulation of deer has eliminated many species of our woodland wildflowers. Personal observation has proven that deer will always eat the buds, twig tips, and newly sprouted leaves of shrubs, bushes, and trees first. In eating the new twigs,

the deer nip them off using their lower front incisor teeth and the gristly pad in the top of their mouths. Because the deer don't have opposing front teeth, the twigs are not clipped off cleanly as a rabbit would do, but are torn off, leaving a ragged, fibrous edge indicative of browsing by deer.

The deer usually feed upon twigs no larger in diameter than a wooden match or $\frac{3}{32}$ of an inch. As these are newly sprouted twigs, they are very high in protein, up to 30 percent, according to the species, and contain little indigestible fiber. Where deer are overpopulated, it is the constant removal of these new twigs that creates the browse line that we see over most of their range.

Browse lines are indicative of a deer population that has exceeded the carrying capacity of the land. (Len Rue, Jr.)

---

thirteen months, the jawbone of the young deer is fully formed to accommodate the third molar, and the fawns finally look like adult deer.

The spring metabolic increase is caused by photoperiodism and is not a result of warmth. The occasional March snowstorm is more of an inconvenience than a hardship because it usually melts away in just a few days. The problem winter is the one that doesn't know when to quit; it just stays cold, the snow doesn't melt, and the deer die. When there is no warmth, there is still the increased need for food on the part of the deer, but no stimulus for plant growth. The deer now need an average of eight pounds of food per one hundred pounds of body weight per day and can't get it. The northern deer yards become bone yards.

If the weather moderates, as it usually does, the does will be the first to venture from the yards. If it snows, the deer will often turn around and return to the yards for a few days. Gradually, the does go farther and farther from the yards and begin to drift back to their respective summer home ranges. The bucks usually follow along about one week later.

All through the winter, the bucks have survived

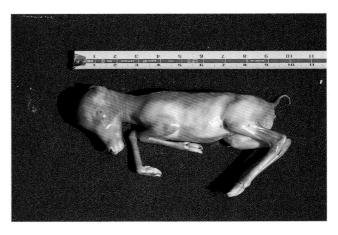

A ninety-day-old whitetail fetus. The fetuses grow slowly during the winter months but develop rapidly when the deer's metabolism increases in March. (Len Rue, Jr.)

If the snow is not too deep, the deer will paw through it to feed on the grasses. (Leonard Lee Rue III)

on the periphery of the yards. Being larger bodied than the does, the bucks require more food, but they can handle coarser vegetation more efficiently and are able to find more food on the outer fringes of the yard. This reduces competition with the does for the food available within the yards.

The winter of 1960–1961 was one of the hardest winters that I have ever seen in my home area of northwestern New Jersey. We had sixty-three inches of snow with about twenty-eight to thirty inches on the ground most of the winter. The temperature plummeted as low as minus twenty-nine degrees Fahrenheit and did not get up to thirty-two degrees Fahrenheit for eighteen consecutive days.

As chief gamekeeper for the Coventry Hunt Club, I had planted acre patches of rapeseed throughout the club's lands. In March, the deer that were alive streamed out of the mountains and cedar patches into the fields and dug down through the snow to feed upon the rape. This cabbage type plant kept many of our deer alive until green-up, although we did lose hun-

dreds of deer that were not able to get to the fields.

The survival of one big buck through that bitter winter was a real surprise and proved again the tenacity for life that all wildlife possesses. Big bucks often stand upright on their hind legs in order to eat vegetation that the smaller deer can't reach. Through either a hunting or an automobile accident, this buck had lost a hind foot right below the hock joint. He was not able to stand up on his hind legs to feed, yet he survived.

In the south, March is spring, and although the deer seldom suffer from winter food shortages, they too welcome all of the newly sprouted vegetation.

APRIL

Although March may be a treacherous month, April is spring. Spring is a time of catch-up for the deer that survive the winter, as they try to rebuild their bodies, to make as large a deposit as possible in their dietary bank books.

There has been a tremendous amount of research

A fraternal group of bucks. Note that only one of the bucks has cast his antlers, proving that bucks cast their antlers on an individual basis. (Len Rue, Jr.)

done on the dietary advantage to humans of eating sprouts. It has been proven that the nutritional value of most sprouts is fifty or more times higher than that of the seeds themselves. This advantage benefits all creatures, including deer, that eat newly sprouted seeds, browse tips, and vegetative growth in the spring. And eat them, the deer do.

With the advent of warmer days, the deer change their feeding patterns and social life. The bucks split apart from the does and do not associate with them at all unless they happen to be feeding in the same area. The fraternal groups of white-tailed bucks in the forested areas tend to consist of no more than four or five individuals. These groups will usually be of mixed age because the hunting pressure takes a heavy harvest of most buck age classes. Even the oldest, most dominant buck eschews the solitary life because fraternal grouping offers a better chance of survival. The more noses, eyes, and ears, the more readily potential danger can be discerned before the danger becomes much more than just a threat. In the more open grassy areas of the western plains and southwestern brush country, the buck fraternal groups tend to be larger. I've seen up to eight bucks together and have heard of as many as seventeen in a group in Texas.

Aggregations of doe groups may be large where they are feeding together in open areas. The maternal hierarchy has now been reestablished in the family and each group is usually led by the oldest doe. The size of such maternal groups varies, but they usually consist of the dominant doe, her daughters, and their offspring. Occasionally four generations will be represented if, for some reason, the granddaughters did not breed or lost their fawns. When a doe's daughters reach their fourth year, they usually become matriarchs of their own groups.

All members of the cervidae family—deer, elk, moose, and caribou—have four-chambered stomachs with the first section, the paunch or rumen, acting as a storage compartment. This configuration allows these animals to gather a lot of food rapidly, minimizing the amount of time they are out in the open, with their attention focused primarily on feeding, and thus exposed to predation. The time required to fill their paunches varies according to the type and availability of the food they are eating.

Ruminants fill up their paunches and then retire back into protective cover to chew their cuds and

Deer have basically five feeding periods per day. This number changes according to the time of the year, temperature, the weather conditions, and whether or not hunting seasons are open. However, in spring, summer, and early fall, if the deer are unmolested, they will generally feed heavily and be active between 2 and 3 A.M. During the 2 to 3 A.M. feeding period, the deer usually don't go back to their daytime bedding area, but there is a lot of movement from field to field. Because this is a time when most of us are asleep, the heavy feeding goes on relatively undetected. Deer also tend to feed heavily around 5 A.M. and then travel back to their bedding areas around 6 A.M. Most hunters are very familiar with this movement because it usually falls within the hours allowed for hunting.

If there are any hills in the area, the deer are likely to bed near the crest of the hill, because the thermals that start to rise between 7 and 8 A.M. will carry the scent of any potential danger up to them. In cold weather, they tend to bed on the south-facing slopes for warmth; in hot weather they will bed on north-facing slopes where it will be much cooler out of the sun's rays.

Unless heavy hunting pressure prevents their doing so, most deer become active and feed again between 10:30 and 11:30 A.M. Because they feed right in their bedding areas at this time, they do not come out into the open and so are seldom seen. Many hunters do not know of this period of activity and so miss out on the hunting opportunities it provides.

The deer again become very active and move from their protected bedding areas to the open areas to feed from about 4:30 to 7:30 P.M., which is the heaviest feeding period. During hot weather, this period will be pushed back. In the south, the feeding periods are both earlier in the morning and later in the afternoon, although the 11 A.M. feeding period remains the same. There is another heavy period of activity between 10 and 11 P.M.

If there are any hills in the area, deer will bed down near the ridges during the daytime. (Len Rue, Jr.)

process the food they have eaten. They have special jaw muscles that allow them to move their jaws in a rotary fashion sideways so that the rear molars can finely grind their food. Deer never eat just one food but instinctively know to vary their diet. Even when eating mainly acorns, they will eat some coarse food for roughage.

On the average, deer will be active between one and one-half to two hours in their two main feeding periods each day and about one hour or less in each of the three minor feeding periods. If food is plentiful, they can fill their paunches in about forty minutes. The rest of the time, 60 to 70 percent of the day, deer bed, chew their cud, sleep, and groom. Although they may not feed when they get up, deer seldom remain bedded for more than forty-five minutes at a time. Then they get up, perhaps to urinate, defecate, or stretch, and may either just turn around or take just a few steps and lie down again. Because the food they eat is high in roughage, the deer must process a lot of it and void feces on the average of thirty-six times a day, approximately once every forty-five minutes, in the summer. In the winter, on restricted food intake, the deer void twelve to thirteen times in twenty-four hours. Deer can void feces while bedded, but they can't urinate; to do that they have to get up.

In the last week in March or the first week in April, photoperiodism signals the pineal gland to cause an increase in gonadotrophic hormones, which stimulates the antler velvet to start laying down the matrix that forms the new growing antlers.

I had always believed that the old antlers had to be cast before the new ones could start to grow since that is normally what happens. I also believed that the pedicle had to be covered over with velvet before new bone salts could be laid down. Not so. In 1997 I saw photos of two different captive bucks that had started to grow new antlers around their old antlers. In both cases, the new antlers were freaky, non-typical, as they had to grow out and then up beneath the old antlers. As the new antlers attained more growth, they eventually pushed the old antlers off.

Antlers are bone, consisting mainly of calcium, phosphorus, magnesium, and other minerals. Although some of the minerals are taken directly from the food the deer are eating, most are catabolized from the buck's own skeleton, causing the bucks to develop osteoporosis during this period. The minerals can then

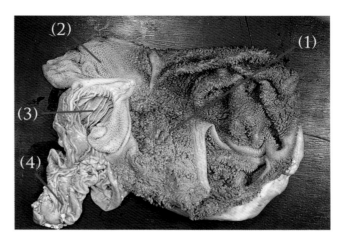

Details of a deer's stomach: (1) rumen, (2) reticulum, (3) omasum, (4) abomasum. (Leonard Lee Rue III)

The shape of fresh deer droppings are a clue to the type of vegetation the deer are currently eating. These pelletized droppings are the result of the deer eating coarse browse. (Leonard Lee Rue III)

be restored to the skeleton over a longer period of time.

Supplied with blood from the deer's superficial temporal arteries, the antler buds start to swell as the twenty-two to twenty-four arteries in the growing antler begin to lay down the minerals, the bone salts, on top of the pedicles. Because the velvet is rich in blood vessels, the antlers are hot to the touch, the velvet having an external body heat of just slightly less than the deer's internal body core heat of one hundred one degrees Fahrenheit.

Antlers are one of the fastest forms of growing tissue, and those of a mature buck grow as much as one-quarter inch per day. As the antlers grow very rapidly,

Left: *Most deer in the northern half of the United States start to grow new antlers the last week of March or the first week in April. (Leonard Lee Rue III)*

Below: *The antlers of a whitetail buck on a good diet will grow as much as quarter of an inch per day. (Leonard Lee Rue III)*

All photos: *Non-typical antlers such as these may be an inherited characteristic or the result of injury to the antler. (Len Rue, Jr.)*

they remain soft and are easily damaged. To minimize any injury to their antlers, the bucks greatly restrict their activities, moving no more than they have to in order to get food and water. While their antlers are growing, the bucks are seldom seen, and the uninitiated observer might be led to believe the bucks have left the area. They haven't.

To help prevent damage to the antlers, the hairs on the velvet stand straight out, and this makes the antlers appear much larger than they actually are. The hairs on the deer's velvet act as a radar system, similar to the whiskers on most predators; they inform the animal of how close it is to everything in its environment. If the antler is damaged and the velvet torn, valves in the arteries, just below the burr, close and stop all surface bleeding. A sebum is produced along-

It was previously thought that the white-tailed deer were basically crepuscular animals, being primarily active at dawn and dusk. Now telemetry studies and a study of deer-truck accidents, as seen in the accompanying chart, show that the deer are basically nocturnal. I'm not sure that this was always so, but as our human population has expanded explosively, and with the unending hunting pressure of the 1800s, deer may have been forced to become more nocturnal than they were in pre-Columbian times.

The accompanying chart was put together for me by my good friend, Mark Stallings, who is head of the risk management department for a large, nationwide trucking company. Fearing that the chart might be skewed because more trucks move at night, he assured me that their trucks moved constantly, consistently twenty-four hours a day.

Three-year study of automobile-deer accidents and the times of day they occurred. (Chart and data © Mark A. Stallings)

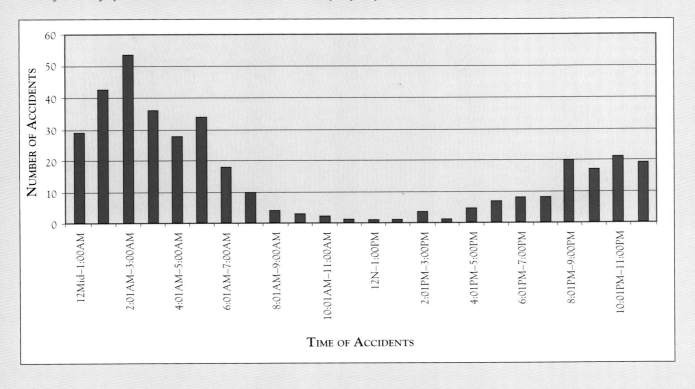

side the velvet hair follicles, which gives the antlers their sometimes "shiny" look. The sebum also acts as an insect repellent to prevent excessive blood loss to biting flies and mosquitoes. It has been claimed that the sebum also gives off pheromones that are an attractant to does. If this is true, it does not produce the desired results because the does keep themselves apart at this time.

Small tears in the velvet heal with no damage. Severe damage to a growing antler may cause the deer to produce non-typical antlers. If the pedicle itself is damaged, the buck may produce non-typical antlers for the rest of his life. Non-typical antlers are not fully understood by deer researchers; sometimes they are a genetic condition, other times they are the result of injury. I have seen a typical buck have non-typical antlers for just the one year in which the injury occurred and then go back to being typical for the rest of his life. Dr. Anthony Bubenik, a Canadian deer researcher, claims that antlers have a "trophical memory" whereby an injury to an antler one year is remembered for the rest of the buck's life.

I have a display board that has ten sets of antlers from a buck that a friend of mine had in captivity.

When the buck was a yearling, it caught the right antler in the fence and broke the antler, which afterward grew with a downward turn and back up. The pedicle was not damaged. When the buck was two and one-half, the antler still grew downward and then back up. For the remaining eight sets of antlers, the right antler grew outward at almost a normal angle, but it always retained a kink in the main beam that lessened slightly each year, proving that the injured antler did indeed have a memory.

It is well known that the right part of the brain controls the left side of the body and vice versa. In deer, an injury to the leg on one side of the body shows up as malformed antlers on the opposite side. This condition usually manifests itself for the rest of the deer's life and is known as a contralateral condition. (Although a buck with a freak antler usually has ex-perienced an injury to the hind leg on the opposite side of the body, R. Larry Marchinton has documented deformed antlers on the same side of the deer's body as a front leg injury.)

I have seen the contralateral condition a number of times and have been able to document it on two occasions. In the one instance, the buck had lost the lower half of his right hind foot, just below the meta-tarsal gland. From the appearance of the clean cut, the foot looked like it had been cut off by a mowing machine while the buck was still a fawn. The deer did not walk on the foot at all. When I photographed him, he looked normal in every other respect except for his antlers. The buck had a good main beam and three points on the right antler while the left antler was a stubby malformed mass.

I would also like to note that it was apparent that

Above: *The right main beam of this buck's antler was broken near the base, and the resultant growth caused it to be a non-typical. (Leonard Lee Rue III)*

Right: *The loss of this buck's right hind foot caused his left antler beam to become malformed. (Leonard Lee Rue III)*

This buck's antlers are growing rapidly and have split for the brow tines. (Leonard Lee Rue III)

the deer was crippled when he walked because the stump of the leg was too short to touch the ground. However, when the buck ran, he appeared to be able to run and jump just as fast and far as any of the other deer. His greatest loss was to his line-up in the hierarchy. His stunted left antler relegated him to the bottom of the list. The loss of his foot also prevented him from fighting and breeding; his loss effectively neutered him.

MAY

May, even in the northern states, is a time of profuse vegetative growth. Deer all over have food in abundance, even in areas of overpopulation. Although the deer are feeding ravenously and filling out their bodies, replacing weight they lost over the winter, and looking less gaunt, they still look "ratty," as they have since the last of March.

The deer's winter coat of hair was bleached to a very light sandy color because of the extreme exposure to sunlight as the deer tried to stay warm in the winter and early spring. The hollow hairs of the winter coat are very brittle, and many of the hairs have broken off. In May, the winter hair falls out in earnest, causing an itching sensation that keeps the deer rubbing and grooming. Shedding starts on the deer's

body behind the elbow and then on the neck, and, as the deer can't lick this area itself, the deer spend lots of time social grooming each other. This grooming may be done by the doe with her fawns or with her grown daughters. The hair loss on the neck will not be replaced immediately, so the neck appears much smaller, making the head appear much larger. The flanks are the next area to lose hair. Sometimes a deer removes the hair right down to the bare skin, and people who see this often think that the deer has mange.

As most of the hair is lost by licking, the deer often eat large quantities of it. They undoubtedly get some minerals by doing this. Usually the eaten hair passes right through the deer's digestive system, but occasionally hair balls accumulate in the stomach. Action in the stomach compacts the massed hair into what are known as "bezoar" stones. Magical qualities were attributed to these bezoars years ago, and they were highly prized as talismans by hunters throughout the world. Due to the amount of hair that each deer ingests, these hair balls are probably quite common but are usually overlooked because most hunters don't look through the contents of the paunches of the deer they shoot. The bezoar stones are usually found in the deer's reticulum and apparently cause no harm.

Deer usually aren't considered territorial, but just

prior to giving birth at the end of May, does do stake out a "birthing territory." The actual size of the individual doe's territory depends mainly upon the overall population of the herd. If deer are abundant, a doe may be able to claim no more than six to eight acres. With a low population, the doe may be able to maintain as much as twenty acres. The quality of the territory depends largely upon the doe's social status. The dominant doe will be able to claim, and defend, the area that has the best cover, food, and access to water and that will be relatively free from predators. The real estate value declines apace with each doe's lower social standing.

The doe's defining of the boundaries of her birthing territory produces the greatest traumatic stress to which her last year's fawns have ever been exposed. The caring mother who guided their every movement for almost a year will now no longer accept them but instead drive them away with slashing hooves. Up to this time, the fawns have been a part of a social system in which they were followers. Suddenly they are beset on all sides, not only by their mother, but also by all of the other adult does in their matriarchal group. The yearlings cannot trespass on the does' territories and are forced to travel whatever corridors exist between them. Before the yearlings were lead, now they are driven. They must seek out their own feeding and bedding areas, and, as the best ones are already taken, they have to travel more and farther. Because of their more extensive traveling, the number of automobile-yearling deer accidents soars during the latter half of May and June. Without their mothers to tell them to look both ways before they cross the street, they are in peril. This increase in traffic fatalities is documented in the accompanying charts.

Because the adult bucks become more reclusive at this time of the year, their proportion of the traffic accidents goes down. That will change in late October and all through November, during the rutting season.

Throughout May, the bucks' antlers grow rapidly. Looking back in my records that I have kept over the years, I find that, by the third or fourth of May, most of the antlers of the mature bucks are four to five inches in length and are splitting for the first time. By May 15 to 18, the antlers are ready to branch again into four points, and by May 29 to 31, the beams are branching yet again, making six points.

Antlers grow like twigs, adding new growth at the tip (not like a grass, which adds growth from the base). The tip of the antler has what is known as the epidermal cap. As this cap has new material added to it, it leaves behind a mineralized cartilage known as the spongiosa or soft bone. As the antler continues to grow, the basal spongiosa begins to calcify, to solidify. The softer spongiosa at the core acts like a shock absorber, allowing the antlers to give a little without breaking. Therefore, while the antlers have an outer cylinder of hardened bone, they still have the spongy core and can sustain great impact without breaking. Contrary to what might be expected, antlers become more brittle as they become more solid. Although bucks do more fighting at the beginning of the breeding season, they actually break more tines later in the season when the antlers are most solid, just before being cast.

Research has turned up some additional interesting facts about deer's antlers. The actual hardness of the bone varies within the antler, with the tips of the brow tines being the hardest of all. Each succeeding tine is less hard. There are two reasons for this differential. The brow tine, being the first tine to be formed, has a longer period in which to harden. In addition, each succeeding tine places a greater demand on the buck's skeleton, and, over time, fewer minerals are available to build antlers.

JUNE

June is a quiet time of year for mature bucks, as they try to keep activity to a minimum in order to protect their antlers' growth. For does, however, June is a tumultuous time, as they deliver and begin to nurture new fawns.

After selecting her birthing territory and driving off her last year's fawns, the doe maintains the territory by aggressively driving off all other deer. It is debated as to whether or not she has a pre-selected spot in which to give birth, but from personal observation I believe that each doe has. One first-time mother that I photographed would get up from her preferred spot and go lie down in a swampy area in order to cool her feverish body, but after just a few moments, she would come back to her original spot, where she finally birthed her fawn.

Thirty-six to forty-eight hours before giving birth, the doe's udder begins to swell to the point that it is readily seen at quite a distance when viewed from the

The explosion of the deer's population coincides with the explosion of our human population, an offshoot of which is that there are more automobiles on the road. That all results in an explosion in the number of deer-related traffic accidents, and the dramatic increase is a major thrust behind society's demand that our deer herds be reduced.

According to the Insurance Information Institute, there are now more than 500,000 deer-car collisions each year. In some states, this represents an increase of more than 100 percent in the decade from 1985 to 1995. In Pennsylvania alone there have been more than 48,000 accidents in just one year. All of these accidents result in more than $1 billion in total damages or more than $2,000 per accident. It really doesn't take much damage to our modern cars to run up a bill of $2,000. A far greater cost is

that more than 200,000 people are injured and more than 200 killed each year in these accidents.

The area in which I live has an estimated deer population of thirty-five deer to the square mile. I have been unfortunate enough to have killed twelve deer with a car over the years. I have been most fortunate in that I have never been injured in one of those collisions. In most cases, the damage to the vehicle was minimal, but after one accident I was left stranded because it was six weeks before I got my Volkswagen van back from the repair shop. Some of my neighbors have been involved with many more accidents involving much greater damage. One friend of mine had the entire deer crash through the windshield into her lap, causing her to total her car in the accident and sending her to the hospital.

Above: *Three deer were killed when this doe and her twin fetuses were struck by an automobile. (Leonard Lee Rue III)*

Below: *Three-year study of the number of deer-related automobile accidents per month. (Chart and data © Mark A. Stallings)*

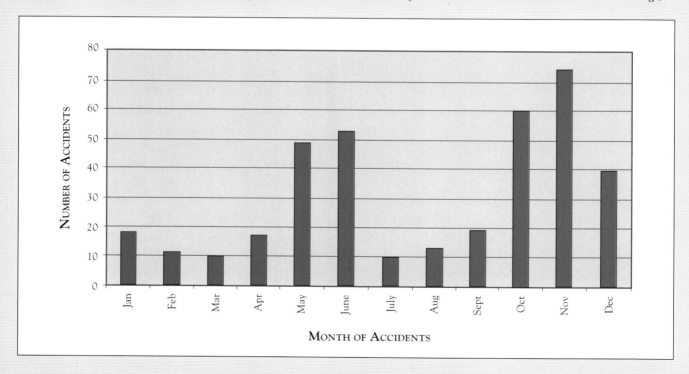

rear. She becomes quite secretive, not venturing out into the open areas, not even to feed, if she doesn't have to do so.

The actual birthing time varies from one to four hours, depending upon whether or not the doe has given birth previously. First-time mothers are usually in labor longer because it takes longer to dilate, and first-time mothers usually give birth to singletons instead of twins. As a rule, singletons will average eight to nine pounds, while twins average five to seven pounds apiece. Naturally, the doe has to dilate more to give birth to the larger fawn.

Very little has been written about the labor pains wildlife go through because birthing is so seldom witnessed. The first-time doe that I mentioned above was a captive doe, and, although habituated to people, she was not tame in the sense that you could get close to her. She passed her water bag around 9 A.M. and did not give birth until 1 P.M. While in labor, she moaned, she groaned, and when she pressed mightily the fawn's front legs would project from her vagina. She would get up and the fawn would slide back in. As mentioned, she would cool off and then come back to her preferred spot and go through the moaning, the pressing, and the getting up process again and again. It was the hardest birthing I have witnessed.

When a doe is about to give birth, she usually turns around and around while standing, till she passes her water bag, which may or may not break upon being expelled from her body. After passing her water bag, she generally lies down and strains and pushes to move the fawn out the birth canal. As the fawn emerges from the vagina, she will stand up so the weight of her offspring helps in the delivery. (Standing during birthing procedure is the norm for all of the cervidae and bovidae females.)

Almost all mammals are born head first because the body is tapered and there is less resistance in this position. Occasionally a breech birth occurs where the fawn is born rump first. Mature does can usually pass a fawn in this position. A first-time doe would be unable to pass a singleton in this position and would probably die in the process, although I have never seen it happen.

The doe keeps her fawns in the birthing spot for a period of six to seven hours while she nurses and washes them and cleans up the area. The fawns can stand in twenty minutes, walk unsteadily in about an hour, and are ready to travel six to seven hours later. The doe then leads the fawns away, using a low grunting to urge them to follow her. She leads fawns two hundred to five hundred feet from the birthing area and hides them apart from each other by about two hundred feet or more. She will keep the fawns apart until they are about three weeks old. After bedding the fawns, the doe will go several hundred feet farther from the fawns and remain hidden herself.

The doe comes back to the fawns three and possibly four times at most per day, and each fawn drinks about eight to twelve ounces of milk per nursing. The doe knows the approximate location of her fawn but not the exact spot, because the fawn may have gotten up and moved a short distance since the last nursing. The doe calls to the fawn with a low, short grunt. The fawn, upon hearing its mother, jumps to its feet, gives a mewing cry, and dashes to the doe. The doe sniffs the fawn carefully before allowing it to nurse, as she will not accept another doe's fawn, although every fawn will attempt to nurse every doe. While the fawn is nursing, the doe licks its anal region, which stimulates its bowels, and the doe eats the feces. If the fawn urinates, the doe licks the urine up. When the fawn is done nursing, the doe will lick the milky froth from around its mouth. No "milk mustache" for fawns.

No living thing is completely odorless, but a newborn fawn is as close as anything can get. As the doe cleans up all excrement, that odor is eliminated. The fawn travels but very short distances, so it leaves only a very short trail of interdigital gland scent.

After the fawn has nursed and been groomed, it leaves the doe and seeks out a secure hiding place on its own. The doe does not bed the fawns; the fawns do it instinctively. I have noticed fawns duck beneath the broad leaves of a skunk cabbage plant and lie curled up beneath, completely hidden by the broad leaves. I have watched blacktail fawns in California do the same thing under bracken ferns.

When the fawns feel they are completely hidden, they hold their heads high and are extremely alert. Their ears swing back and forth as they focus in on each sound in their environment. At even the earliest age, the fawn's ears are tuning in and filtering out sounds that don't represent danger. They hear but pay no attention to the wind soughing through the trees, the rustling of the leaves, the quick hopping in the leaves of squirrels and chipmunks, the high overhead drone of an airplane, or the distant roar of traffic, because they are constants. If anything other than its

Shortly after the doe's water bag breaks, her straining causes the gradual emergence of the fawn's front hooves. Note that this fawn's feet are still partially enclosed in the bag, which still contains some of the amniotic fluid. The white hoof tops are a soft cartilage that does not tear her vagina.

Not having dilated sufficiently, the doe lies down. Her constant straining pushes the fawn's forefeet, head, and shoulders out of the birth canal.

Once the fawn's chest emerges, the doe usually rises to her feet, utilizing the fawn's weight to help pull the fawn from her body.

The doe immediately gets up to investigate the fawn, which may or may not still be wrapped in the amniotic sac. She frees the fawn from the sac, pulling the membrane loose with her teeth. She does not attempt to eat the sac at this point; she just wants to make sure it is off the fawn's nose so it can breathe.

The rough tongue-washing that the doe gives the fawn cleans off the blood and residual amniotic fluids that would definitely attract predators. In the process, the doe is covering the fawn with her own saliva, which will help imprint her on it. The same licking, tasting, and smelling is bonding the fawn's own odor to the doe because the doe cannot recognize her fawn by its voice; she will recognize it by its odor.

The doe's constant turning causes the fawn's body to swing like pendulum, back and forth, and this motion helps in the birthing. Once the fawn's hips are out, the hind legs come out in a rush. Because of the stretched-out length of the fawn, it doesn't have far to fall and is not injured.

I am firmly convinced that the dropping of the fawn and the rough washing stimulates the fawn's body processes to start functioning, much as slapping a human baby's bottom does.

Within ten minutes, the fawn is seeking the doe's udder and moves by flopping around. By the time the fawn is twenty minutes old, it is making straddle-legged attempts to stand. The fawn falls frequently until it gains some semblance of coordination.

The second fawn is usually born twenty to thirty minutes after the first. The doe goes through the entire procedure of the straining, standing up, turning around, lying down, and getting up, only this time the fawn is born so much easier because the doe's birth tract is already fully extended. Some does don't even stand up to use the second fawn's weight to pull itself free; the fawn just quickly slips out of her body.

Immediately after giving birth to the second fawn, the doe concentrates all of her efforts on it, again removing the amniotic sac as fast as she can. While she is engrossed in this effort, the first fawn is still struggling to its feet.

After twenty minutes, the first fawn has gained its feet and is attempting to nurse while its mother vigorously washes its sibling.

Now the second fawn gets to its feet while the first fawn is nursing. Within a half hour, the second fawn, too, will have been washed and has started to nurse.

While the second fawn lies down and rests, the first fawn continues to nurse. The doe continues to lie down to facilitate the fawn's nursing, and all the while she is constantly licking one fawn or the other, whichever happens to be the closest to her. This nursing and washing goes on for about three hours.

During the vigorous licking, the doe covers the fawns with her own saliva, which will help the fawns imprint on her. At the same time, the tasting and smelling of the fawns imprints the fawns on her.

While the fawns are resting, the doe is pulling the afterbirth from her body with her teeth.

The doe turns her attention to eating the afterbirth. Every vestige is eaten, providing the doe with additional nutrients and perhaps helping stimulate milk production. The doe then eats every bit of vegetation that was splashed with the amniotic fluid and blood, everything from the grasses to the dead leaves, including vegetation she usually avoids. For example, deer ordinarily don't eat the leaves of the skunk cabbage, yet I watched a doe eat every leaf of several plants because they had been splashed with the birthing fluids. She will then even eat some of the soil.

The fawns, at two hours old, are quite steady on their feet, but rest frequently.

It is very important that the doe nurse the fawns while lying down during this first period because some of the fawns may be too weak to be able to nurse while standing. It is also very important that the fawns get all of the very thick, super-rich colostrum milk that the doe produces the first three days of nursing. This colostrum milk contains the antibodies to all of the diseases to which the doe has ever been exposed, and she passes them on to the fawns through the milk, inoculating them. The whole milk we buy in the store has a butterfat content of about 3½ percent. As most of us are now weight conscious, we prefer milk that has only 1 or 2 percent butterfat. The milk that whitetail does produce ranges between 10½ to 12 percent butterfat, and on this rich diet the fawns strengthen and grow very quickly.

By the time the fawns are four hours old, they are strong enough to follow after the doe, and she leads them away from the birthing area.

The doe leaves each fawn in a different bedding area so that they were separated by about one hundred feet. This separation reduces the likelihood of a single predator discovering both fawns. The fawns will be kept separate for up to ten to fourteen days.

(All photographs by Len Rue, Jr.)

mother approaches, the fawn drops its head to the ground, curls up in a tight ball, and folds its ears back along its neck; its eyes remain open, but the fawn is motionless.

The fawn's bright russet-red coat has slightly more than three hundred white spots, allowing the fawn to blend in with the sun-dappled leaves on the forest floor, providing a perfect cryptic camouflage.

I can not give a better description of what happens next than to quote from what I have already written in my book, *The Deer of North America*.

Nadine Jacobsen, of Cornell University, did some very interesting research that has added greatly to our knowledge of fawns and their physiological activities during the first week of life. She put radio telemetry equipment on five fawns that monitored their heartbeats and breath rates. A newborn fawn, at rest, has a heart rate of about 177 beats per minute. This rate drops to about 130 beats per minute at two weeks and is down to 102 beats per minute at one month. An adult deer at rest averages about 37 beats per minute. The fawns had unrestricted use of a large pen with natural vegetation and were observed constantly both visually and by telemetry. Their reactions to various stimuli were recorded.

Phase I was considered to be a fawn, undisturbed, resting. Its head was up, its ears were forward. It averaged 177 heartbeats and 21 breaths per minute.

At phase II, an unfamiliar observer approached the fawn. The fawn put its ears back, dropped its head, curled into the prone position, and remained motionless. Instantly, within just one beat, the heart rate dropped from 177 beats per minute to 60 beats per minute. In 53 out of 74 tests, all breathing was suspended.

At phase III, as the observer sat quietly about 1 yard (1 meter) from the fawn for a short period of time, the fawn's heart rate crept back up to 102 beats per minute and it began to breathe normally.

At phase IV, when the unfamiliar observer again moved, the fawn's heart rate instantly dropped again, to 82 beats per minute, and breathing was again suspended.

At phase V, after the observer left the fawn, its heart rate went back up to 183 beats per minute and its breathing went up to 30 breaths per minute. The higher rate is undoubtedly an effort to repay the oxygen debt incurred during the alarm period.

As the fawns grew older, their normal "resting" heart rates decreased when tested and, conversely, the abnormally low heart rate at phase II increased. After five weeks, the fawns responded to an alarm stimulus with increased breaths per minute as they prepared to run to safety.

The survival benefit of the slowed heart rate is tremendous. The drop was so sudden that in a split second the fawn literally went into suspended animation or pseudo-hibernation. All body functions slowed down so that the brain was not deprived of oxygen, nor could the slowed heartbeat be heard. During the period of suspended breathing, the breaths could not be heard nor was there any exhaled carbon dioxide to be smelled.

The doe, meanwhile, has removed herself from the area to prevent her own body odor from attracting predators to her fawns. She usually is within hearing of the fawns, although she may be out of sight. If a dog, coyote, or other predator appears in the area, the doe may either try to lure it away from the fawns or, in some cases, may actually attack. A determined mature doe, using her slashing forefeet, is a formidable defender.

When humans approach the fawns' area, the doe usually remains hidden. If people should inadvertently find a fawn, they often assume that since they do not see the hidden doe the fawn must be an orphan. Conservation officers and rehab centers are usually over-

Facing page, top: *One-day-old fawn hiding. It has dropped its head, curled up tightly, and folded its ears back. The fawn will remain motionless in this position until the unidentified noise it has heard goes away. (Leonard Lee Rue III)*

Facing page, bottom: *An alert one-week-old fawn. When they feel they are safely hidden, fawns keep their heads lifted, constantly monitoring each sound of their surroundings for danger. (Leonard Lee Rue III)*

whelmed each June when these misguided, uninformed folks pick up the "orphans" and take them in to care for them. If you should ever discover a fawn, **DON'T TOUCH IT, DON'T PICK IT UP, LEAVE IT BE.** The fawn is not an orphan unless it's found close to where a doe is lying dead, having been killed by an automobile.

After five to six days of age, the fawns will usually run if they are approached, and, at this age, they can easily outrun a human.

Because the fawns have been moving around each day, a little farther each day, they soon learn the limits of their mother's territory, and, if they do run, they will run in circles in order to stay in an area they know.

After eighteen days, the fawns will follow and bed with their mother. At about three weeks, the doe gives up her birthing territory, and the matriarchal groups will re-form. Now most of the yearling does will also rejoin the group, while up to 50 percent of the year-ling bucks will have dispersed to new areas and either formed or joined up with other fraternal groups of bucks.

It is in the fawn's first two weeks that predators take their greatest toll. At the Wilder Wildlife Refuge in Texas, research has shown that in some years coy-otes take up to 70 percent of the fawn crop. Bob Avery has told me of extensive fawn loss due to coyotes in parts of New York's Adirondack Mountains. In 1996, I witnessed heavy coyote predation in my home area of northwestern New Jersey. (Losses to coyotes in my area have lessened, as an outbreak of mange in the coyote population in 1998 has reduced their number

Above: *This doe in her bright russet-red summer coat is nursing her week-old fawns. (Len Rue, Jr.)*

Facing page: *In mid-June, the buck's antlers are still growing and many are already a large size. (Len Rue, Jr.)*

a little.) Black bear populations are exploding in many states, and the bears prey heavily on fawns. Bobcats and dogs take their toll. Only in Minnesota, Wisconsin, Michigan, and Canada are there enough wolves to be a menace to deer.

By mid-June, the main beams on a mature buck will be twelve to sixteen inches in length, and the antlers will be branching for their fourth points. Including the hairs, the base of the antlers' main beams will be more than two inches in diameter, making them look very impressive.

The deer's winter coat has now been completely removed and replaced with the short, thin, bright russet-red summer coat. The summer coat is designed mainly for insect protection. Numerous flies of different types plague the deer. The flies particularly bite the area on the bridge of the nose from the nostrils to the eyes; this area has almost no hair on it. The deer, while bedded or standing, turn and rub their heads against their bodies or against their legs. They often use a hind foot to scratch their heads and remove the flies.

Over most of the county, vegetative growth reaches its peak, in both production mass and protein, in June. Those deer not feeding on farm crops are feeding mainly on forbs, which they much prefer over grasses, although they also eat the latter. Although lactation in the does and antler growth in the bucks are caloric expenses, the sufficiency of the food covers these expenditures with enough left over to allow for good body growth.

July

July means heat. The sun's rays that speed up the growth in vegetation cause most wildlife to slow down, especially in mid-day. All over the country, the deer don't move until the setting sun causes the trees to throw long shadows across the fields, and then the deer start their feeding in those shadows.

Deer pant through their opened mouths to expel body heat rapidly, just like a dog. There is no hair on the deer's ears in the summer, and the ears act as thermoregulators, cooling off the blood as it courses through them, just like an elephant. The blood vessels in the buck's growing antlers cause not only the antlers' mineralization but also body heat dissipation. However, the deer's greatest defense against the heat is to move as little as possible, and they move only when it's the coolest part of each day.

In the southwest, the Coues and Carmen Mountain whitetails are exposed to searing heat and usually seek relief by going up on top of the highest elevation in their areas. In the southwest, the temperature is high, but the humidity is low, so creatures that can find good shade are usually quite comfortable because the heat causes thermals that create cooling breezes.

In the southeast, the high heat is usually coupled with high humidity, and, where possible, the deer seek out wet areas where rapid evaporation can cause some comfort in the shade.

Over most of the rest of the country, the respiration of the trees' leaves causes the forest to be cooler than any of the surrounding areas, as the sun causes water evaporation from the leaves. Wherever there are streams flowing, the motion of the water causes the temperature to be slightly lower, and the deer are quick to take advantage of all of these conditions.

All spring the difference between the warmed earth and the cooler air temperature at night causes a heavy condensation of dew to accumulate on all vegetation. The dew, combined with the succulence of the growing vegetation, usually produces enough moisture to supply the deer's need so that they don't have to drink much water. That begins to change in June, and the maturation of many plants in July reduces their water content. In July the deer usually go to water at least two times each day, drinking two to three quarts each time. Deer are almost never found more than one mile from some water source. In my area of northwestern New Jersey, I doubt if any deer has to travel more than one-fourth of a mile to reach fresh water.

In July many of the deer start to feed in ponds and lakes. Feeding in the water not only helps to cool the deer off but also gives them relief from the many biting insects. In the far north, the ponds and lakes are especially important to the deer because the black flies and mosquitoes are a torment beyond belief. Also, in mature conifer forests, the ponds and lakes are the major openings in the canopy, allowing the sun to produce a profusion of food. Water plants, particularly the broad-leafed water lilies, are very high in minerals. As rain leaches minerals from the soils of the entire area, the water carries the dissolved minerals to the brooks and streams, which in turn deposit them in the ponds and lakes, where they are picked up by the roots of the water plants. The deer also eat a lot of the

Above: *From mid-summer until late fall, deer go to water two or more times a day and drink two to three quarts of water a day. (Len Rue, Jr.)*

Right: *Deer get a lot of the moisture they need by eating plants covered with dew. (Uschi Rue)*

filamentous algae, those long, green, gossamer strings of vegetation growing on the water's surface. All of the algae are very rich in proteins.

I have noticed that deer feeding in the ponds and lakes readily feed with their heads submerged in water up to their ears. Although I have seen deer feed with their heads completely submerged, they really don't like to do it and seldom do. Deer want their ears to be above water so that they can listen for potential danger.

Each day, as the shadows lengthen, the matriarchal groups of does, their fawns, and some of the yearling bucks that are tolerated within the group begin to filter out of the daytime cover to feed in the more open fields. The fawns still get almost all of their food through the milk they drink, but all of them are also

Above: *By playing and gamboling about, fawns build up the strength and endurance that is needed for their survival. (Len Rue, Jr.)*

Right: *Deer feed heavily in ponds in July and August to get relief from the heat and flies and to feed upon the mineral-rich vegetation. (Leonard Lee Rue III)*

Facing page: *Like this buck, most deer escape detection by simply remaining motionless, hidden by brush. (Len Rue, Jr.)*

tasting, testing, and eating some vegetation. Because the fawns don't have to spend all of their time actually feeding, they can spend much of their time in play, and play they do.

All play is a conditioning for later life. The running and jumping exercise the heart's ability to pump more blood faster, increase the lungs' capacity, and build muscles. Lactating does seldom take part in this summer play. The yearling does and bucks may be tempted to join in, running and dashing about because they are younger than the does and are not subject to the drain of lactating.

From close observation over hundreds of hours, I have noticed that the fawns play the same games that many of us played when we were kids. The fawns actually play tag; they run and chase after each other, but on many occasions they actually touch, "tag," the fawn they are chasing. I have seen this happen too many times to label it coincidence; it can only be labeled tag.

Fawns also play hide and seek. They race about and then dash into cover, remaining hidden until they are "found." This training is extremely crucial to their survival, because research has proven over and over again that most deer escape from hunters by remaining hidden and letting the hunters walk on by them.

For instance, in one research project eleven bucks were released in a one-mile-square fenced enclosure. Ten hunters were allowed in to hunt each day. They were not allowed to gang up and put on drives but had to hunt by stalking or standing while researchers watched with binoculars from towers the interaction of the deer and the hunters. In most cases, the bucks just bedded down and remained motionless. One buck lay hidden in the brush of a fallen tree while the hunter sat on the tree trunk and ate his lunch. Other bucks were seen to circle behind the hunters and follow them. One buck was observed getting down on his knees and crawling away. No bucks were killed at all on the first day. So much for "shooting fish in a barrel," as some had said it would be.

In addition to playing, and it often seems to be a part of playing, fawns are beginning to assert their dominance. This assertion usually occurs first among siblings, but the striking out with the forefeet and the occasional head-butting soon hammer out a dominance hierarchy among all of the fawns.

I postulate that if a doe gives birth to a pair of twins of both genders, the female, by receiving more testosterone from the bloodstream she shares with the male, will be a more dominant doe in later life. Although this theory begs for more research, other recent studies have shown that female mice have more testosterone in their bloodstreams if they were positioned between male fetuses in the uterus than if they were positioned between females. Increased testosterone in either a male or female system usually increases aggression.

The mature bucks are still very reclusive, and physiological changes have been taking place within their bodies since the summer's solstice around June 21. Now, as the days shorten, the brain starts to increase its production of melatonin, which in turn triggers the entire endocrine system into greater activity. The bucks' testicles begin to enlarge, producing more testosterone, which causes the now nearly full-grown antlers to begin to solidify.

AUGUST

The last antler growth is usually completed over most of the country by the first week in August. The burr grows outward gradually, impeding and then shutting off the flow of arterial blood to the velvet. This decrease in arterial blood flow in turn reduces the veinal blood flow through the antlers' interior, which causes the spongiosa to solidify into bone at the base. The reduced blood flow is immediately apparent because as the velvet dries it loses its mass, decreasing its size and tightening to the antlers so they have the appearance of being "shrink-wrapped."

By the second week in August, the deer's reddish summer hair is starting to be replaced by the tips of the new winter coat of grayish brown hair. Because of the shortness of the deer's summer coat, the transition to the winter coat is not as noticeable, and the deer do not get a "moth-eaten" appearance. It is also in August that the fawns start to lose their spotted coats, through a combination of some of the hair tips breaking off and the complete shedding of the hair.

In August the does begin to wean their fawns in

Antlers begin to harden from the base toward the tips. By mid-August, the drying velvet at the base of the antler gets a "shrink-wrapped" appearance. (Len Rue, Jr.)

Note the engorged ticks on the body of this white-tailed deer. (Leonard Lee Rue III)

Above: *Deer often lick an itch to get relief, and they remove ticks by biting at them and pulling them loose. (Leonard Lee Rue III)*

While bedded, this buck uses his antlers to scratch an itch. (Len Rue, Jr.)

earnest. The fawns have been fully functioning ruminants since June. Most does allow the fawns to nurse a little for at least four months. Really tolerant does may allow the fawns to nurse until they are six months old or older. From three months on, a doe's milk supply diminishes, although the milk's butterfat content goes up slightly. The lessened supply of milk is not an impediment to the fawns' growth because they are constantly increasing their intake of vegetation. However, fawns orphaned before two and one-half months of age are not likely to survive.

The deer evidently have a high need for nitrogen, as is shown by their preference for nitrogen-fixing le-

gumes such as alfalfa, clover, peas, and trefoils. All of these crops are also very high in proteins.

Deer do their greatest damage to corn in the spring when it is about six to ten inches high. By nipping off the terminal leaders, they prevent that stalk from producing an ear of corn. However, deer do the most damage to farm crops as a whole in the month of August because most of the natural vegetation has matured and dried and its food value has dropped sharply. Many of the farm crops are still succulent, especially the hay crops that have been mowed and have regrown. I have always said, "You are what you eat." This axiom applies to wildlife as well as to humans. The best nutri-

Occasionally deer misjudge the height of a fence and get their feet caught in the top wire. Unable to free themselves, they die there. (Leonard Lee Rue III)

This buck died as a result of getting his antlers wedged in the crotch of a tree he was trying to rub. (Len Rue, Jr.)

tion comes from the best plants grown on the best soils. Many of our soils are worn out, depleted of minerals through poor farming practices. Good farmers apply fertilizers and use irrigation to produce better crops. If you fertilize a five-acre patch in the middle of a twenty-acre field, deer will feed more heavily on that five-acre patch because the vegetation is better and their instinct instantly recognizes that fact.

In the south, and to a greater degree in the southwest, August often produces drought conditions. Lack of rain reduces all vegetative growth, and a drought may be as deadly to southern deer as hard winters are to northern deer. Southern deer do not gain noticeably in weight in the summer as do the northern deer because the excessive heat causes them to greatly curtail their activities.

Southern deer are subject to more parasites and diseases than are the northern deer because the extremely cold weather in the north kills most of the external parasites. The really great surge in the population of southern deer herds occurred only after the federal government's screwfly eradication programs were put into place. Adult screwflies laid their eggs on the umbilical cords of newborn fawns. The larvae then invaded the fawn's body through the navel, and in some years most of the fawn crop was wiped out. Ticks, particularly the Lone Star tick, are one of the main scourges of the southern deer today. Tick control is being accomplished in the south by baiting the deer with corn laced with pesticides, although controlled burning is still the most effective tool. Controlling the parasite load on cattle by running them through dip tanks also helps the deer.

A disease that kills large numbers of deer is the epizootic hemorrhagic disease caused by two types of epizootic viruses and five types of the blue-tongue viruses, all of which produce the same symptoms. The name describes the disease's action; infected deer die from actually hemorrhaging blood through the walls of their arteries into organs of the body. The disease is transmitted by biting midges and does not affect humans or livestock. It reappears annually in some of our southern states. Frost puts an end to the midges and curtails the disease until the following year.

I am personally well acquainted with the disease because in 1975 it hit particularly hard on the farm right next to my property. The Kopycinski's farm had a tremendous herd; before the epizootic, it was common to see seventy-five deer feeding in just one field.

Lyme Disease

Like their southern counterparts, northern deer have ticks, and the one that has gotten the greatest attention is the tick *Ixodes dammini*, which carries the spirochetes *Borrelia burgdofer* that causes Lyme disease in humans. Although the disease was first diagnosed in northern deer, it has since been found in most sections of the country. The disease has spread and will continue to spread because we have far more ticks today than we did forty to fifty years ago. Prior to that time, farmers and ranchers often burned off the high dead grass in fields. In an effort to reduce air pollution, Environmental Protection Agency (EPA) rules now prevent burning, but the resulting high dead grass provides perfect habitat for ticks. It is most unfortunate that the tick is known as the "deer tick," because it is probably spread more by mice than by deer. More than forty species of birds also are known to host this tick, and the disease has been spread rapidly throughout the country by these birds. Lyme disease does not affect the deer or any other wildlife; they are just the host animals.

Lyme disease can be easily treated with antibiotics, such as Doxycycline, if diagnosed properly and early. If not treated, it can cause paralysis and even death. Fortunately a Lyme disease immunization has been discovered and is now available to anyone under the age of seventy. I don't know why the age of seventy was the cut-off point, but as I am seventy-three, I can't get it although I live with deer all year long. I will continue to do what I have done for the last fifteen years and what I would advise you to do. I periodically saturate all of my pants and socks with Permanone, a permethrin concentrate developed for tick and insect protection by the federal government. It works and is a lot cheaper than the vaccine, and it is available to anyone at any age.

The epizootic killed dozens of deer from the herd, greatly curtailing the number of deer in the area.

In addition to being plagued by various parasites and diseases, the deer infrequently have natural accidents. As discussed, the most common accident befalling deer is collisions with motor vehicles. In their wild dashing through the woods when threatened by danger, the deer sometimes impale themselves on sticks. This is uncommon because, if given the chance, the deer will dash off using a trail, and they know where every obstacle is. Occasionally, deer get hung up on a fence when they misjudge its height. In jumping the fence, they clear the top strand of wire with their body, but their feet go under the top strand and thus often get tangled. I have seen this on only a half dozen occasions in sixty years of study, which leads me to believe it is not a common occurrence.

One of the freakiest deer accidents I've seen occurred in autumn 1998. I discovered a beautiful ten-point buck hanging from a pine tree. The tree's main trunk had split about two feet above the ground, and the two trunks were growing about two inches apart. The buck evidently started to rub his antlers on the tree, and the curve of his left main beam slipped in between the two tree trunks. Just the slightest change in body position locked his antler between the trunks.

In his panic at not being able to free himself, the buck must have thrashed around just a bit, as the leaves were kicked away from the tree's base. However, his frantic efforts were so forceful that the left antler beam broke a large piece of his skull plate, which punctured his brain, killing him. That he died quickly was shown by the fact that the earth was not torn up as it would have been in a long struggle.

It was merciful that the buck died so quickly because he had no chance of freeing himself. When I found him, he had been dead about a day. After my son and I had photographed the buck, I cut the skin around the broken antler, and the deer's body dropped away. Even then, we could not pull the antler up out of the crotch of the tree. I had to cut one side of the tree crotch with a chain saw in order to get the antler for my collection.

SEPTEMBER

September witnesses a tremendous surge of activity in the deer. Gone is most of the summer's heat and with it the somnolent, lazy days of inactivity. Photoperiodism is the master plan; the testosterone coursing through the buck's body is the driving force. In all deer the shortened hours of daylight trigger the feeding frenzy demanded by lipogenesis. The weather cooper-

Above: *In the northern two-thirds of the continent, most bucks rub the velvet from their antlers during the first week in September. (Len Rue, Jr.)*

Facing page: *A buck's antlers are darkest in coloration just after the velvet has been removed. (Len Rue, Jr.)*

ates by dropping the temperature just enough to allow the deer to move much more actively, for longer periods, without being stressed. It also helps that, although the deer's summer coat has been replaced by the winter coat, the new hairs have not grown out to provide maximum insulation as yet. The fawns have shed their spotted coats.

Usually in the last week of August and the first week of September, the bucks begin to peel the velvet from their antlers. Mature bucks often peel four to five days earlier than the younger bucks, but I have seen younger bucks peel first on many occasions. Whereas up to this point the bucks have done everything possible to avoid hitting their antlers against anything, now they rub saplings vigorously. My very dear friend and mentor, Joe Taylor, told me that he watched one of his captive bucks completely remove the velvet from his antlers in just ten minutes. He said the buck's ac-

tions were frenzied. The buck started to rub against a sapling, then whirled around and grated his antlers against the fence, and then went back to the sapling. Joe also said that he had seen some of his bucks take up to three days to get all of the velvet off their antlers.

The shortest time I have ever seen it take a buck to remove the velvet was just a little over one hour; most of the time it takes at least twenty-four hours. Frequently the velvet is removed from the main antler beam but hangs in shreds at the base. These shreds infuriate the deer because they flap back and forth in front of his eyes every time he moves and interfere with his vision. The buck will vigorously rock his head back and forth, trying to shake the strips of velvet off. He will try to catch the strips with his mouth and pull them off. I have videotaped bucks using their hind feet to try to scratch the velvet loose.

Bulking Up

Each autumn, the deer go through a period of mandatory lipogenesis; they must consume all of the food possible to put as much fat on their bodies as is possible. If food is plentiful, the deer will continue with both body growth and the build-up of fat. If food is scarce, the fat build-up will continue at the expense of restricted body growth. This situation often causes confusion among hunters. When they see fat stored in the body of their deer, they assume the deer is getting an adequate nutritious diet or it wouldn't be fat. Most folks don't realize that that fat is there despite inadequate food and comes at the expense of current smaller body size and, in the case of bucks, of smaller future antler size.

If there is a good crop of acorns, or the deer have access to plentiful farm crops, such as corn, soybeans, and apples, they will go into the winter in good shape. Deer fatten faster on acorns than on any other food. In a good acorn year, the deer's kidneys will be buried in fat, there will be skeins of mesh fat surrounding the intestines while globules of fat, like fistfuls of cherry tomatoes, will be stored between the pelvic arch. There will be layers of fat under the deer's skin, covering their entire body. There will be layers of fat interlaced throughout their muscle tissue. A deer in such condition has a surplus of funds in its bank account and, if it does not have to unduly exert itself, can go up to two months without eating, and survive.

A deer with this amount of stored body fat could go sixty days without eating and survive. (Mark Wilson)

On a number of occasions, with both whitetail and mule deer bucks, I have seen the bucks start to rub the velvet but not complete the job. With several of the deer, it looked as if they had not even attempted to remove the velvet; it had just dried and split. With others the velvet was partially removed, but many dried, curled strips still clung to the antlers, and the bucks made no attempt to rub them off.

I have read many accounts where the authors said that a buck's antlers are pure white after the velvet is removed and that the antlers darken as they are stained by the sap of the trees they are rubbed against. This is contrary to everything I have witnessed over a lifetime of observing deer. The antlers of all of the bucks I have ever seen were darkest just after the velvet peeled, stained by the residual blood that was in the velvet. I'm not saying that some additional color is not added by tree sap because some may be. However, a buck's antlers are colored equally over their entire surface, and this equal coloration could not happen by rubbing on the sap, as the buck cannot possibly rub every part of his antlers against a sapling.

Apples are a favorite food of deer, and the deer get to know the location of every apple tree in their area. (Leonard Lee Rue III)

Deer will forsake all other foods to glut themselves with acorns. (Leonard Lee Rue III)

Acorns are the number one preferred food of the white-tailed deer. Clockwise from upper left: red oak, white oak, and chestnut oak acorns. (Leonard Lee Rue III)

Contrary to what has sometimes been printed, I find that a buck's antlers gradually whiten as they are constantly exposed to bleaching by sunlight and leaching by rain. Just prior to being cast, the antlers are almost pure white.

After the velvet is removed from their antlers, the mature bucks continue to rub trees, although their main focus for the next month will be feeding.

By September, the weaning of the fawns will be completed. The fawns still try and would actually continue to nurse if the does would allow it. Fawns in nursing suck and pull down on the teat, but to increase the flow of milk, they also butt up into the does' bags. When the fawns are small, the butting is not too hard, but as the fawns grow larger and their lower incisor teeth grow bigger, the pummeling of the udder can be painful. In weaning, the does may allow the fawns to suckle for a moment or so, but then the does usually get the fawns off the teats by stepping over their heads and walking off. Or the does may refuse to let them suckle at all. Weaning not only forces the fawns to eat more vegetation but also puts an end to the does' lactation. This is critical to the does' own survival, as when the drain of lactation is lessened the does can then begin to build up the fat reserves on their bodies.

With the advent of cooler weather, the fawns increase the amount of time spent in play. They run, they jump, they buck in the sheer exuberance of life. I have seen them buck and jump so wildly that they often lose their balance and fall. The fawns' spontaneity is so contagious that the does often join in, running and dashing about at full speed. The yearlings are usually the first to join in, but even the older, more sedate does temporarily forget their matronly ways and join in the fun.

The social life of the deer changes dramatically in September. Whereas up to this point the bucks usually kept themselves separate from the matriarchal groups, they now often mingle with the does. This is not a sexually driven grouping, as it will be later, but is merely a concentration on the greatest food supplies.

As mentioned so frequently, deer know their home range intimately, including exactly where all of the various types of food are located and when each will be available. Deer know where all the berry bushes are and when the berries ripen. They eat not only the tiny twig tips in the spring, but they also love the berries. They know where all of the fruit trees are and practically catch each apple or pear as it drops. A hard windstorm may drop an overload of fruit that will soon ferment in the warm sun. I have seen dairy cows get drunk on fermented apples. A few years ago, Massachusetts had to close its bear hunting season to give the drunken bears a chance to sober up. I can imagine deer might also get intoxicated on fermented apples, but I have never seen it happen. Perhaps it is because there are too many deer to allow any one deer to get enough of the fermented apples.

In the third and fourth weeks of September, the acorns begin to drop. In some years, such as 1998, the acorn crop is fantastic; in other years it is sporadic. Red, black, and chestnut oaks usually drop some acorns every year while the white oaks may have a good crop only every three to four years. Although the chestnut oak acorn is the largest of all the acorns and usually quite plentiful, the deer don't favor them as they have a high tannic acid content and are bitter but will eat them after they have eaten all the others.

Deer have no gall bladder; most of their food is so low in fat content that they do not need the bile to process it. Acorns are high in fat, but the deer usually feed on them for only three or four weeks until they are all eaten. (The squirrels, turkeys, raccoons, some ducks, and the bears also feed heavily on acorns, further reducing the amount deer will eat.)

In some states, the last week of September also is the first week of the bowhunting season. Novice hunters are often perplexed when the deer seem to have suddenly "disappeared." The deer haven't disappeared, they just don't come out into the open fields to feed as they have been doing all spring and summer. When the acorns, their favorite food, drop, the deer simply stay in their bedding areas or up on the rock benches and ridges and glut themselves. Although acorns are their main food at this time, deer still vary their diet by eating of other types of vegetation; this vegetation makes up about 20 percent of their diet.

OCTOBER

In October, push really comes to shove. Increasing testosterone levels in the adult bucks' bodies bring on a rising level of belligerence that manifests itself in mid-October when their necks swell and the rutting season begins. The testosterone levels in one-and-one-half- to two-and-one-half-year-old bucks rise slower than in the mature bucks; their immaturity produces lower levels of testosterone, and the mature bucks' belligerency depresses and suppresses the younger bucks' libido.

Signposting by making buck rubs begins now in earnest. Like a boxer preparing for a match, the saplings and trees are hooked, rubbed, and grated with increasing force. A mature buck will make dozens of rubs in a twenty-four-hour period. As the constant rubbing strengthens the neck muscles, more pressure can be applied to subsequent rubs. I have seen bucks deliberately entangle their antlers in small saplings and then rip them from the ground. Charles Atlas, who first publicized isometric exercise, would be proud of their efforts.

During October, the mature bucks pull out all the stops in their advertising campaigns—they start to make scrapes. Scrapes are usually made along the edges of fields, along roads, and along the sides of well-used trails. In the south, I have seen scrape lines whereby the scrapes are actually intervisible—by standing at

Above: *By mid-October in the northern areas, the bucks are running at all of the does to get them to urinate. They then can check the urine to see if the does are ready to breed. (Len Rue, Jr.)*

Left: *After the rutting season begins in mid-October, the mature bucks of the north greatly increase their traveling range in search of receptive does. (Leonard Lee Rue III)*

Above: *After the rutting season begins, mature bucks show aggression to all other bucks they encounter. (Leonard Lee Rue III)*

Right: *Bucks within a fraternal group spar almost constantly to determine dominance, but full-fledged fights are rare. (Len Rue, Jr.)*

one, you can see another in either direction. I have not seen this in the north, but then our northern bucks in my area simply do not make as many scrapes as do southern bucks. Scraping peaks among the mature bucks around November 7, after which time they will be too engrossed in actually breeding to spend much time making scrapes. About the time the mature bucks stop making scrapes, the younger bucks start to do so.

The bonds that have held the bucks' fraternal groups together begin to loosen at this time but have not as yet been broken asunder. Younger bucks still run with the mature bucks but make few rubs until

the end of October. The bucks now increase their ranges, traveling miles in search of receptive does. Although the bucks are capable of breeding the does, the does are not capable of accepting them, so much of the rubbing allows the bucks to work out their frustrations. The bucks also seek sexual relief through masturbation, a common enough occurrence with many types of wild creatures.

It is during the middle of October that the fraternal groups break up, with the mature bucks traveling alone. I don't know who said, "He who travels alone travels fastest," but the big bucks believe it. They cover

lots of ground, searching for estrus does, challenging rival bucks, asserting their dominance when they can, eating little, and moving at all times of the day and night. Mid-October is the beginning of the peak time for hunters because the bucks are moving more and respond more readily to grunt tubes and antler rattling. They respond because at this time of the year these are bucks with an attitude. However, I want to assert again that where hunting pressure is heavy the really big trophy bucks do not throw caution to the wind, they do not run around willy-nilly during the daylight hours. They got to be trophy bucks by using

their smarts, and they know it's not smart to run around during the daylight hours when they can be seen. At this time of the year, there are more hours of darkness than of daylight, and most trophy bucks will only move under the cover of darkness. Trophy bucks don't move during the daylight hours unless someone pushes them out of areas in which they have chosen to stay hidden.

From the October on, the bucks start to run the does. When a buck encounters a doe, he runs toward her with the same aggressive posture with which he would challenge a rival buck. The main difference is that although the head and neck are held down and

The mature bucks will usually have the biggest bodies and the biggest antlers. Both of these qualities make them the dominant bucks. (Leonard Lee Rue III)

forward, the ears are also held forward, and the tail is often raised. In challenging another buck, the ears would be flattened back along his neck, and the tail would be clamped down tight.

Mature does respond by quickly squatting and urinating because at this point the buck is interested only in checking their urine for the pheromones that denote estrus. Often younger does simply dash away when they see the buck running at them—a futile response because the buck will chase them until they stop and urinate.

Bucks in fraternal groups almost never fight because dominance has long since been established and

is constantly reinforced by sparring. Most of the sparring is done by the yearling males. They push and shove each other many times each day, testing, testing, testing. You can tell that they are putting little effort into it because their legs are straight under their bodies. In fighting, the bucks' legs are always angled sharply backward to provide power and the base from which to push. Occasionally, even the mature bucks spar—it's only sparring unless one gets hooked and hurt, and then it may turn into serious fighting. It is a commonly accepted practice for the younger bucks to spar with the mature bucks as part of their training. They do this often and are tolerated. The big bucks know that

There is often heated debate about the benefits and drawbacks to using commercial deer scents in hunting. In my opinion, any hunter or photographer who is not using scents while hunting or photographing deer is missing the boat. Scents are not a magic potion with a guaranteed success, but they are another aid because, as I've mentioned, deer live in a world of scent.

First and foremost, let me remind you that so long as you live and breathe you cannot completely eliminate human odor. You can only minimize it. Don't eat spicy, garlicky foods; anything that taints your breath heavily will also ooze out through the pores of your skin. Wash with a non-scented soap, such as Ivory, and do not use scented deodorants, after-shave lotions, or toilet waters of any kind.

Keep your hunting clothing clean by washing it in baking soda or Sport Wash. Do not wash your camo clothing in any of the modern detergents that have ultraviolet (UV) brighteners; they will make your clothing glow in the UV segment of the color spectrum, which the deer see. (See chapter 2.) When not in use, keep your hunting clothing packed in a clean plastic bag with some pine or cedar branches or pine scent. It was a common practice for Native Americans to stand in the smoke of a sweet grass fire before hunting, so that their clothing would absorb the natural smells and cover their own human odors. Eating chlorophyll tablets can't hurt, but goats eat lots of chlorophyll-filled grass, and you can still smell them. Take all of the above precautions, then make sure you are downwind of where you expect the deer to be, and you should be okay.

As a cover scent, I have found that fox urine works very well. It is an odor that deer encounter all the time, as foxes mark their territories as often as dogs urinate on car tires, and fire hydrants and foxes pose no threat to deer. (There have only been a couple of recorded instances of foxes attacking newborn fawns.)

Food attractant lures work very well for the deer in early October, especially apple and acorn concentrates.

I would not use an estrus lure before mid-October, when the bucks actually expect to encounter it. Any odor used out of season might make the bucks suspicious.

Regular deer urine works well at all times as either a cover scent or an attractant. I have found that buck urine works well because every big buck wants to check out every new buck scent in his area. (It's a macho thing; the boss buck wants to make sure that all other bucks know he's boss.)

Hunting downwind from a major scrape is one of the best tactics that can be used in bowhunting. Every buck that passes through the area will check it out. Adding buck urine makes the scrape even more effective, for the buck that made the scrape will check it to see what competition has passed through the area. If there is not a scrape in the exact spot you want it to be, you can create a "mock" scrape, and the bucks will use it. The mock scrape was first tested and written about by my good friend Bob McGuire. The key to the success of the scrape was an overhead branch.

Using cotton swabs on a stick, Bob removed saliva from the mouths of harvested deer and rubbed it on the overhead branch. Using a deer foot, he scraped the leaves away beneath the branch, creating the bare earth patch that was needed and in the process adding interdigital gland scent. Then he liberally poured buck urine in the scrape, and the bucks accepted the mock scrape as their own.

Bob and other researchers, including myself, have found that the easiest way to get bucks to accept and use a mock scrape is to remove the overhead branch from a current scrape and fasten it over the spot where we want the mock scrape to be. The key seems to be that the overhead branch must be chewed upon, which leads me to believe that the saliva is more important than the forehead scent gland; it evidently is more individualistic. As already mentioned, the bucks mark overhead branches all year long, but they only chew on the overhead twigs during the rutting season. In moving the overhead branches, I always use new gloves that I have liberally rubbed with fresh dirt. I use fine wire that I also rubbed in dirt to suspend the branch over the mock scrape; string always retains an odor of its own and should not be used.

Above: *This dominant buck was badly injured when an opponent's antler tine pierced his skull. After being injured, even yearling bucks gored him. (Len Rue, Jr.)*

Left: *Bucks often circle each other trying, by using body language, to get their opponent to back down. (Leonard Lee Rue III)*

the younger bucks are only practicing because only an equal animal would truly fight a big buck and because the younger bucks do not display the body language of aggressiveness. I have often seen five-month-old buck fawns, with no antlers visible, spar with the big dominant buck. The fawns often do this while the big buck is lying down, the big buck just twisting and turning his head a little in response to the fawn's effort. When the big buck tires of the game, he will swing his head more sharply and rap the little guy with an antler, denoting that play time is over.

Ordinarily the biggest-bodied buck will also have the biggest set of antlers and will be the dominant buck in the entire area. The exception to this is when the biggest buck is getting on in years, say nine years old, and starting to go down in strength. Then a much younger buck, being in his prime at four or five years of age, will be much more aggressive, although he does not have either the body or antler mass of the older buck. In that situation, the younger buck's youth, vigor, and aggression will allow him to dominate the older buck.

If the dominant buck is injured, his descent on the hierarchical ladder is determined by the extent of his injury. I once witnessed what had been a dominant buck being chased and gored by a six-point buck. It was immediately evident that the big buck had been injured because he could not run. The big buck stag-

gered down the hill and crawled under the branches of a downed tree, lying part way in a small brook. A short time later a small spike buck came along and rammed his spikes into the big buck's rump until he tired of the sport. When I checked out the big buck, who died shortly thereafter, I found that he evidently had fought another big buck, and his rival's antler tine had punctured his skull plate and had gone into the brain. The fight must have occurred hours before I found him because pus was already oozing from the wound.

I have found the reaction of the spike bucks to be so typical. For all kinds of wildlife, including birds,

when a once-dominant creature is injured, all of the lesser-ranked members get in their licks as they try to kill him so they can move up the ladder a notch.

Fights occur when two dominant bucks from rival fraternal groups meet. Such confrontations occur when the bucks leave their home range and increase their traveling over their much larger breeding range. Although the dominant bucks are perfectly willing to fight, they much prefer to have a rival buck acknowledge their dominance by running off. If both bucks display the hard stare and neither runs off, a fight is imminent. Continuing the hard stare posture, with all body hair fully erect, the bucks circle each other at a

Although fighting bucks are each trying to kill the other, that seldom happens. Only nearly equal animals fight, and evenly matched competitors make it difficult for one to prevail. (Leonard Lee Rue III)

Fighting bucks come together with explosive force, and the battle then becomes a pushing contest with each trying to throw the other off his feet. (Len Rue, Jr.)

I am quite sure that this buck was not killed by the buck he was fighting. I believe a third buck hit him from the side during the fight. (Leonard Lee Rue III)

When hunting, rattling antlers works to attract deer because every buck and many does are interested in seeing which bucks are fighting, and, in the case of the bucks, they may want to do battle themselves. Rattling works in all parts of the country with both whitetail and mule deer, but it works better in the south than it does in the north, because there are more mature bucks in the south.

The effectiveness of rattling antlers was first shown to me by Tom Fleming of Maryland, the man who is an expert at rattling antlers and who first publicized rattling as an aid to hunting. In November 1983, I had been the keynote speaker at the Dixie Deer Classic in Raleigh, North Carolina. Fred Bear, Dr. Rob Wegner, Dick Idol, myself, and others were at a reception in Dr. Carroll Mann's home when Tom was persuaded to show us his rattling technique. Fred asked me what I thought, and I said it was a good show, but I'd like to see it work in the field. Tom agreed to prove it, and prove it he did the following deer season.

We went out on public land in Virginia—land that was open to heavy public hunting pressure, not some private preserve. The days were not really good because they were windy; deer don't like to move in the wind, plus the wind makes it hard to get the sound to carry to the bucks. Despite all the handicaps, Tom did succeed in rattling in four bucks in three days, with the best buck being a six pointer. What was fascinating to me was that none of the four bucks came charging in; they all tip-toed around in a circle, trying to see the fight without having to be a part of it. Tom advised using medium-sized antlers for rattling. He said that using big antlers will call in big bucks if there are any in the area but often scare the average buck away. Large antlers produce a lower sound, and the deer can guesstimate the size of the buck by the sound of his antlers. Using medium-sized antlers will attract all bucks.

Some time later, I was doing photography on a Texas ranch. Seated on a hill, my guide and I had a good view of the fairly open range land. When my guide crashed a set of antlers together, one big buck jumped the fence and came charging right in, while several smaller ones circled around.

Tom Fleming was the first to prove to me that "rattling" deer really works. (Leonard Lee Rue III)

This superb Texas buck came in to the sound of rattling antlers expecting a fight. (Len Rue, Jr.)

distance of about fifteen feet with a stiff-legged gait, grunting loudly. They are so perfectly attuned to one another that when one buck turns to charge, the other buck's charge is a mirror image.

The bucks charge with all the strength and speed they can muster. Although either of the bucks may be injured in the initial collision, because they are equal animals their antlers are usually about the same size and come together without either animal having the advantage. After the initial impact, the entire fight is an attempt to throw the rival off his feet and to gore him. Both bucks put forth their best effort to do this to their rival and to prevent this from happening to themselves. Although only equal animals fight, one is usually more equal than the other, and the other realizes this in just a few moments.

From personal observation, I would say that most fights are over in less than ten seconds. Most of the fights I have witnessed were over in five to ten seconds; some lasted up to one to two minutes, while the longest might have been as long as five minutes. I have read of fifteen-to-twenty-minute fights and seen photos taken of such fights. Fights seldom last that long because the bucks can't last that long; the effort the bucks put into the fighting is just too exhausting.

When one of the two bucks realizes that his rival is stronger, he breaks away and dashes off. The victor seldom follows for more than one hundred yards. He is not now interested in killing his rival, although he would have done so just a few moments before in the fight. Now he is content to have proven his dominance.

One exception to this occurred in Pennsylvania about eight years ago. I heard antlers crashing together in the distance and knew a fight was in progress. I was up on the top of a hill and knew that there was no way I could carry my big video camera down the hill and up over the top of the next hill in time to record the fight. Suddenly I heard the sounds of snapping branches and a running deer. I set my tripod down and got my camera ready. A big buck, his tongue lolling out of his mouth, burst over the hill and headed for the pond below me. The buck waded body-deep out into the pond and sucked in water, but he kept looking back over his shoulder. Following on his trail came the buck that had just bested him in the fight. When he saw that he was still being followed, the first buck hurriedly exited the pond and dashed in a circle back up the hill he had just come down, with the vic-

torious buck right behind him. The victorious buck did not appear to have as large a set of antlers, but he appeared younger than the buck he was chasing. I am sure it was a case of a younger, more aggressive buck toppling the dominant buck from his pinnacle. I am equally sure that he intended to kill him if he caught up with him. I'll never know what happened for sure; they disappeared from sight and hearing and were gone.

I did photograph a big buck that was killed in a fight, but I do not believe he was killed by the buck he was fighting. The buck was killed by a third buck, who charged at him from the side. The third buck's antler deeply punctured the initial buck just behind the rib cage and angled up through his lungs. Wildlife has no concept of "fair play." Might makes right, and when animals fight, they fight to win by any means at their disposal. Many, many times, with all kinds of hoofed animals all over the world, I have witnessed two animals fighting head to head when a third male would charge in and hit one of the combatants in the side or in the rear. The animal being struck has absolutely no chance to defend himself against such an attack; most times he doesn't realize it's happening until he is hit, and then it is too late.

Rarely, but only rarely, two bucks lock antlers while fighting and are not able to free themselves. Under the initial impact, the antlers spring apart slightly and then snap back together. When both sets of antlers spring apart, if they are evenly matched, they may slide inside of each other's tines and in snapping back may lock together. Bucks that are locked together usually die of starvation, lack of water, and stress. The ones that die quickly are the fortunate ones. Occasionally one buck dies and the other drags it around until he finally succumbs. I read of one buck that was found dragging a carcass that had been partially eaten by coyotes. The terror the surviving buck must have felt by not being able to flee from the predators can only be imagined.

When bucks that have been locked together have been found in time, they have sometimes been saved by a person sawing one of the antlers off. There are a number of cases where a rescued buck has charged the people who have just rescued him. Always use caution if you should ever attempt to help such locked bucks.

While doing a program in a school in Black Earth, Wisconsin, I met the principal, who showed me his most prized possession. On the corner walls of his of-

Despite having broken his left main beam, this Texas buck maintained his dominant position because of his aggressiveness. (Len Rue, Jr.)

fice, he had the mounted heads of three bucks that had had their antlers locked together and had died. I have read of two additional instances of this happening.

Antlers are frequently broken in fighting, and more break later in the season as they become dry and brittle. My friend Joe Taylor saw two bucks fight, and when they collided one buck's antler snapped off near the base, arcing through the air for about seventy-five feet. Needless to say, that was the end of the fight.

I videotaped a dominant buck in Texas that had half of his right main beam broken off in a fight. He also had a gaping puncture wound in his neck. Either condition should have lowered his status in the hierarchy, but it didn't. That buck was as aggressive as he had always been and challenged or chased every buck he encountered. He had psychology working for him. He had evidently beaten all of the other bucks so badly when his antlers were perfect that none of his rivals were willing to test him so long as he maintained his

aggressiveness. This was a most unusual situation, and it is the only time I saw a buck maintain his status despite a broken antler beam. Ordinarily, breaking off a main beam or casting his antlers will effectively neuter a buck.

Antlers are not primarily defensive weapons, although bucks will use them to defend themselves if they are attacked. If they were defensive weapons to be used against predators, they would be kept all winter when the deer are most vulnerable. Antlers are sexual weapons used for dominance, and after the breeding season they are no longer needed. The antlers are then cast so that any big buck who has broken tines or main beams can get back in the game with his new antlers prior to next year's breeding season.

NOVEMBER

For bucks over most of the continent, November is their reason for being. They are at their magnificent best; they are ready for the breeding season. About

No one knows why some bucks' antlers sweep out on a flattened plane on each side of their heads while others' antlers go almost straight up. Still others sweep forward and bend inward so that the ends of the main beams almost touch. Some antlers have little "sticker" points, short projections of antler points growing out at the base of the main beam or even projecting from a tine. Drop tines, tines growing out from the bottom of the main beam, are not uncommon.

What we do know is that the configuration, or shape, of an antler is a genetic characteristic, a characteristic that can come directly from the buck or from the doe's genes from her sire. We know that the shape of a buck's antlers is determined before his birth, and the shape will never change. The only thing that changes is the size and mass of the antlers, and that is determined by the buck's age and the food he eats.

While I am interested in the huge, non-typical antlers that some deer produce, I much prefer the clean, simple lines of a perfectly matched set of typical antlers. My idea of perfection in a whitetail's antlers is that, when you look at a big buck sideways, you see only the near antler, as the far antler is identical in size and shape.

Above: *Some bucks have very wide-spreading antlers. (Leonard Lee Rue III)*

Facing page, top: *Other bucks have very high antlers. (Leonard Lee Rue III)*

Facing page, bottom: *With a perfect set of symmetrical antlers, this buck's near antler almost blocks the view of the far antler. (Len Rue, Jr.)*

Above: *Note the whitetail-type antlers and the blacktail crescent-shaped metatarsal gland on this crossbred buck. Whitetail bucks will pursue mule and blacktail does much more aggressively than mule and blacktail bucks do, which leads to cross-breeding. (Leonard Lee Rue III)*

Facing page: *I prefer perfectly symmetrical antlers to non-typical, and this buck represents perfection to me in both body and antler configuration. (Len Rue, Jr.)*

twelve to forty-eight hours prior to a doe's coming into estrus, she becomes very high strung and nervous and starts to move about constantly. She visits buck scrapes that are in her area. She stops frequently and dribbles urine in the trail. She is as anxious to be bred as the bucks are to breed her, but she is not ready just yet. With the bucks almost constantly on the move, it is not too long before she has a number of bucks following the enticing trails she is laying down.

I have read many accounts where the writer advised his hunter readers that if they want to bag a big buck, they need to find the buck's breeding territory. I have never seen any evidence of such a territory. I have always advised hunters to go to the area in which the deer are feeding at that precise time. The does will be where the food is, and the bucks will be where the does are—it's that simple. I don't mean to say that all the deer will be there in a heap—they won't—but

the does will be in the vicinity of the best food available at that time.

One other point I would like to stress is that the does do have a preference for one buck over another. Ordinarily the does prefer the biggest buck, and ordinarily the dominant bucks do the bulk of the breeding. However, several times, in both Texas and Louisiana, I have seen does run from the biggest buck but stand for another buck. It could be that the biggest buck's extreme aggressiveness scared them off.

Years ago, I got a very nice eight-point buck for my very first captive doe. I had them in a five-acre pen that was fenced in eight feet high with four-by-six-inch hog, or woven, wire fence. That eight-point buck was a good-looking buck, but my doe wanted absolutely nothing to do with him. He ran after her constantly, and just as constantly she ran away from him. The night that she finally came into estrus, she stretched the woven wire strands apart and went out through that fence. The next morning I discovered the hole, and, as she had never been out of the pen before, I figured she was gone for good. Not so. Later that afternoon, I stood outside my home with friends and saw the doe coming down the wood road followed by a ten-point buck. We watched the buck through binoculars. He stopped in the road about three hundred feet from the house and would not come any closer. The doe walked right up to me, and, using my belt, I led her back to her pen. The eight-point buck came running up to her, but off she went. She just wanted nothing to do with him.

I didn't realize that we had a big ten-point buck in the area because I had never seen him nor had any of my neighbors. I don't know if the big buck came to the pen at night to visit the doe or if she just smelled him from a distance. I do know that she knew he was in the area, and she wanted nothing to do with that eight pointer.

The following year she did the same thing, stretching a hole in the fence and going through it. Her doe fawn went through the fence after her but did not accompany her when she ran off with the buck. This leads me to believe that her fawn went out the hole after the doe was gone, because the fawn was in my yard, but the doe was not. Contrary to many published reports, every doe that I have seen bred had her fawns somewhere close by. Does in estrus, when chased by bucks, run in a circle to stay in their home range and also to stay close to their fawns. When the doe is chased and runs off, her fawns run with her.

The following spring my doe gave birth to a pair of buck fawns, one of which had eight points as a yearling, and the other had nine points. Both bucks were ten pointers at two and one-half years of age. Although the bucks were twins, it was apparent that they were fraternal, not identical, twins, meaning that they came from two different fertilized eggs. Although the dominant buck's sperm fertilized both eggs, the does genes were as apparent in her offspring as the buck's.

These bucks were as different as day and night. The one buck had a longer body than normal, and his antlers were much more massive and heavy than his brother's, their longest tines never measuring more than nine inches in length. The second buck had what I considered the perfect deer body configuration. His antlers were perfectly matched, and the longest tines were about eleven inches in length, although they did not have the mass of his brother's antlers.

It is a well-known fact that the shape of the dominant buck's antlers will usually be seen in the shape of his offsprings' antlers. The fact that the antlers of these twin bucks were so entirely different, as were their body shapes, shows just how important genes of the doe's sire are.

However, I have always contended that the doe's genes are more important that the buck's, and I'll tell you why. Any buck fawns born to a dominant doe have a better chance of becoming dominant bucks than the buck fawns of the lesser does because they will have a better start in life. He will have first chance at better food and will grow faster and stronger because of their mother's dominance. Their father provides the nature, but their mother provides both nature and nurture, and, with deer at least, the nurture is more important. You are what you eat.

Whitetail bucks are very persistent and aggressive in the pursuit of pre-estrus does, much more so than mule deer bucks, and their persistence and aggressiveness is causing a decline in the mule deer population in some areas of the United States and Canada. It was long thought that mule deer and whitetails would not interbreed, and, if they did, the resultant offspring would be infertile. We now know that both of these claims are false. If both a whitetailed buck and mule deer buck are in the area when a mule deer doe comes into estrus, both bucks will follow her. However, because the whitetail chases harder and longer, he will get to do the breeding. Within just four generations, the mule deer characteristics will be all but non-existent. Today biologists fear that the whitetail will breed the desert mule deer of west Texas out of existence. Crossbreeding is also reducing the mule deer population in parts of Saskatchewan and Manitoba, Canada, and some western states of the United States. However, some recent research shows that, in some areas, the mule deer are increasing at the expense of the whitetails.

Research has proven that if captive does are kept in close proximity to a buck, they may come into estrus as much as ten days earlier than usual. It is thought that the constant odor of the buck triggers early ovulation. Under normal conditions, all of the does run from all of the bucks until their estrus cycle is ready to kick in. Then the constant attendance of the courting bucks will stimulate them.

A pre-estrus doe is soon followed by a retinue of

Note the difference in body size between a mature buck and doe. (Leonard Lee Rue III)

bucks, with the largest, most dominant buck keeping the closest to her and trying to keep all other bucks away from her. The chase is long and hard, and the deer are almost constantly in motion and cover a lot of ground, but because the doe runs in a big circle, they stay in the same general area. This chase goes on for about twenty-four hours until the doe is actually ready to breed.

The dominant buck can usually keep the lesser bucks at bay by just giving them the hard stare. Perhaps he will run at them with a short charge of twenty feet or so that usually ends with his bouncing up and coming down with both front feet. If another dominant buck shows up at this time, a fight is sure to ensue.

When the doe does decide to stand, I believe from personal observation, she picks the area in which she stops. One estrus doe I photographed for two days in West Virginia made circles in about a one-hundred-acre area. I have seen no sign of a buck attempting to drive a doe to a specific area.

Mature bucks go through quite an elaborate courtship ritual. The buck approaches the doe aggressively but is very solicitous of her if she stands. He may groom the doe about the head, particularly around the ears where she also has forehead scent glands. He may lick her flanks and udder. He definitely licks her vaginal area, and this may cause her to hump her back slightly in a position called lordosis, moving her tail to one side as she does. This humping position is a definite indication that she is ready to stand.

The buck will then move behind her in an attempt to mount. The buck usually makes three or four false mounts before intromission actually takes place. In between these false mounts, the buck will further stimulate the doe by vaginal licking, and, in turn, the doe may incite the buck by licking his penis sheath. I do not believe that the false mounts are caused by inexperience or ineptness on the part of the buck. I believe they are part of the ritual needed to cause the doe to ovulate, to release the egg from her ovary into the fallopian tubes to facilitate impregnation. Usually

Above: *A whitetail buck courts a doe by licking her ears. (Leonard Lee Rue III)*

Right: *Copulation of a whitetail buck and doe. (Len Rue, Jr.)*

Does strain mightily after being bred and expel several teaspoons of fluid. (Leonard Lee Rue III)

on the fourth or fifth attempt the buck's penis finds its way into the doe's vagina. Two or three quick thrusts are followed by a deep thrust; ejaculation by the buck is indicated by his almost perpendicular body position with his head thrown back. Occasionally in making this final thrust the buck's hind feet come off the ground, and he falls over backward. The deep thrust is needed to implant the sperm as deeply as possible in the cervix to shorten its trip to the eggs.

Immediately following the buck's final thrust, the doe will spread her legs wide, hump her back, and strain mightily. There are some who claim that this is an orgasmic climax. That may be, but I'm not sure why the doe does it, because in the process she ejects several teaspoonfuls of her own vaginal secretions as well as some of the buck's semen. (I have documented this in video.)

Through years of observation, I have found that most deer breed about every four hours, and you can almost time it. As a doe is in estrus for twenty-six to twenty-eight hours, the buck will breed her on the average of about six times.

As with all males, there are exceptions. I know of one buck that bred a doe about eight times during the daylight hours that I watched them. Undoubtedly he bred her additional times under the cover of darkness. I also witnessed a buck breed a doe twice in fifteen minutes, but such quick copulation is very unusual.

I have never seen a buck willingly share a doe with another buck, although I have been told of it happening on several occasions. I was photographing a tending buck in Louisiana when another big buck showed up. The tending buck immediately charged at the newcomer and chased him farther than usual, and I think he did so because the second buck was big and a potential rival. As soon as the tending buck left the estrus doe, a little four-point buck ran to her and mounted her. Upon seeing the little buck mounting his doe, the tending buck came thundering back. The four pointer had made the ejaculatory thrust just before the big buck was on him. The little buck escaped, but he had to quickly tear his penis from the doe's vagina. It was that or die—the big buck was coming in from the side, intending to put his antlers through the little buck's rib cage.

I was told by some friends who worked for the Hercules Powder Plant in Belvidere, New Jersey, of a "gang rape" of a doe by a group of nine bucks. During World War II, the Hercules Company had purchased five farms for their plant and fenced in the entire area with an eight-foot chain-link fence topped with eighteen inches of barbed wire. The deer herd that was enclosed inside the fence increased in number and size rapidly as no hunting was allowed.

The aforementioned doe burst into view, coming over a hill, closely pursued by nine bucks of different sizes. The doe had a hard job running. Her tongue lolled out of her mouth. She was exhausted and gasping for breath. Every time she lay down, one of the bucks would hook her with his antlers to get her back up on her feet. She was bred by three different bucks in the fifteen minutes she remained in view. My friends said that the bucks showed no antagonism toward each other.

After breeding, the doe usually lies down because she is tired from the constant chasing during the prior thirty-six to forty-eight hours. The buck often will lie down anywhere from 10 to 50 feet from her. There are usually other young bucks in the area, and they will constantly try to move in on the doe. So long as the younger bucks stay at least 150 feet from the doe, the dominant buck just ignores them. Once they come within that circle the big buck will spring to his feet and chase them off. The dominant buck usually just assumes the hard stare position and walks toward the younger buck. When the dominant buck gets to the edge of the 300-foot circle, he may give a short charge at the retreating younger buck, causing him to move further, faster. Then the dominant buck returns to a position close to the doe. He does not attempt to drive the younger buck right out of the area, because if he goes too far from the doe, another young buck may dash in from the other side and attempt to get to her.

This action is repeated over and over again, but it is not constant. In between, the dominant buck may feed a little, the doe may get up and feed a little, and they may both bed and chew their cuds a little. The outrider bucks may also bed and chew their cuds a little

The buck always approaches the doe aggressively during the rut, and it is this aggression that causes her to run at least a short distance. (Len Rue, Jr.)

but only for a short time, and then it's back to harassing the dominant buck and doe.

After about four hours, the dominant buck aggressively runs at the doe again. She will jump to her feet and run off a short distance with the buck in hot pursuit, and then everything is set in motion again. Nothing that I have ever seen will cause such an explosion of deer activity as a doe running past, chased by bucks. Even if a dominant buck is bedded, guarding an estrus doe, he will jump to his feet and often join the frenzy of another pre-estrus doe being chased by other bucks.

There may be some reason for the buck to approach the doe so aggressively, but I can't fathom what it might be. If the dominant buck walks over to the bedded doe, she frequently will reach up and caress his mouth, and he will gently do the same thing to her with what I can only call affection. He may walk around and lick her vaginal area, and that doesn't bother her. It's just when he puts his head down, neck extended, and runs at her that she jumps to her feet and runs off.

While the dominant buck is guarding the estrus doe, her fawns will bed and feed close by. On many occasions I have seen non-estrus does bed down close to the estrus doe. By staying within the buck's protective three-hundred-foot circle, the does are safe from being harassed by eager younger bucks who would run all of the does relentlessly. The dominant buck, by keeping the younger bucks away from the estrus doe, provides an island of peace for the other does and their fawns. Even the yearling bucks will be tolerated in the general area so long as they show no interest in the estrus doe, and some of them don't. Most of them do and are chased.

About 50 percent of all yearling bucks disperse from the doe's home range permanently when she establishes her birthing territory in the spring. The other 50 percent come back and rejoin the family group when the doe's new fawns are about a month old. The yearling bucks that do return are not well received, and they are harassed more and more by all of the mature does in the buck's family group as the breeding season approaches. It is not the dominant bucks that finally cause the young bucks to permanently disperse but the constant attacks by the familial does. As the young bucks usually disperse on an average of three to six miles, they are well beyond the doe's home range, giving them little contact with the familial does and helping to prevent inbreeding.

The final dispersal of the eighteen-month-old bucks, the constant traveling of all of the bucks, and the chasing of the does cause deer-car accidents to peak again between October 15 and November 15.

While it is true that the dominant buck does the bulk of the breeding, it is impossible for a northern buck to breed more than five or six does each fall. There simply is not enough time. The buck is with the doe for twelve to twenty-four hours before she comes into estrus, breeds her during the twenty-four to thirty-six hours that she is in estrus, and usually stays with her for another six to twelve hours before leaving to seek another doe. The breeding season for the northern does—"the window of opportunity"—is narrow, and the does tend to be synchronous, with most coming into estrus at about the same time. If the buck spends a minimum of three days with each doe, he would only be able to breed three or four does over a twelve-day period—a period longer than the peak of the breeding season by at least two days. There will always be a doe or two out of sync with the bulk of the herd, coming into estrus earlier or later but not by much.

Does in estrus are not going to wait around; some buck will breed them, but they will not all be bred by the dominant buck. The breeding season in the south is much longer, so the dominant buck may have a chance to breed more of the does. Bucks in the Texas grasslands try to maintain a small harem of three to four does, something the northern bucks never do.

Does are on an estrus cycle of twenty-eight days. Does that are not bred, and does that do breed but don't conceive, come back into estrus about twenty-eight days later in the first part of November, resulting in what is known as the second rut. Does will continue to cycle until they are bred. (See postscript.) On average, about 95 percent of all mature does do conceive each year.

December
December sees a tremendous transition in the deer's activities as both the year and the deer begin to close down.

Around December 5, the second peak rut takes place in the north, during which the few mature does that did not conceive in November will do so. This is also the time when any seven-month doe fawn that has achieved a critical body mass of between seventy

Where possible, bucks will feed heavily on corn to regain body weight lost during the rut. (Leonard Lee Rue III)

to eighty pounds will probably breed. As mentioned earlier, mandatory lipogenesis occurs at the expense of body growth for all fawns in October where food supplies are low. Where food supplies are plentiful, the fawn's body growth can continue while fat stores are accumulated. In October and November, carbohydrates are critical because they produce fat. After the acorns are all eaten, the deer will switch to corn in areas where they can get it. In Illinois and Indiana, with their abundance of farm crops, about 80 percent of all of seven-month fawns reach or surpass the critical body weight and so are mature enough to breed. Even where food is plentiful, the little does don't usually make this weight in November, which is why almost all fawns, if they attain the needed weight, are bred in December.

That one extra month is critical. In my home state of New Jersey, anywhere from 40 to 60 percent of our seven-month doe fawns breed, according to the availability of food in the different areas. On the rich farm-

The mounting of one buck by another is a sign of dominance. (Len Rue, Jr.)

The growth of the bony pedicles beneath the skin are visible on a six-month "button buck." (Leonard Lee Rue III)

land of Hunterdon and Mercer Counties, about 60 percent of the doe fawns breed. On the mature forested mountain ridges behind my home, in Warren and Sussex Counties, most of the doe fawns do not breed. The same conditions hold true for similar regions of Pennsylvania and New York. In Vermont, New Hampshire, Maine, and other parts of New England, almost none of the doe fawns breed because of the lack of food in the forests and the generally shorter seasons.

Buck fawns start to show what appears to be interest in sexual activity between three and four months of age. I say "appears to be" because the mounting of siblings and peers by little bucks may be just a show of dominance. I have on a number of occasions seen a mature buck in a fraternal group mount another buck as a sign of dominance. The buck's penis was not exposed during the mounting nor was there any thrusting to denote sexual activity. This mounting of subor-

dinates by the dominant males is common to many species of mammals. By November, the buck fawns are definitely showing sexual interest and display it frequently by trying to mount their mothers. This action may be tolerated by the doe, or the little buck may be rebuked with a hard kick.

Except under ideal conditions, most buck fawns do not mature sufficiently to become sexually active their first year. It is generally conceded that a buck is not sexually mature until he is seventeen to eighteen months old. The exception to the rule is where the buck fawns have had access to an unlimited diet of 16 to 18 percent protein. All little bucks grow pedicles on their frontal skull plates, and, by the time the bucks are three months old, these pedicles form into the little knobs that we refer to as "buttons." If little antlers grow on the pedicles, break through the skin, form velvet, peel, and harden during December and January, that buck will also be sexually mature and capable

Research has proven that if a seven-month buck produces little peeled antlers, it has developed enough to be capable of breeding. (Len Rue, Jr.)

of breeding. Because of his small stature, the little buck will be unable to breed an adult doe; he simply can't reach her. He can breed doe fawns, although he would probably be prevented from doing so by the mature bucks.

Hellenette Silver, a research biologist for New Hampshire's Department of Fish and Game, was the first to discover that if a buck fawn had little peeled antlers, he was sexually mature. Silver had a pen of captive fawns that had been fed a high protein diet *ad libitum* (unending). No adult buck had ever been with the fawns, yet the following summer several of the yearling does gave birth. One little buck in the pen had peeled antlers. After Silver wrote a paper about the occurrence, other researchers replicated and confirmed her results. It is very rare for buck fawns to grow antlers.

The rutting season comes to an end around December 15 in the northern two-thirds of the United States, just as the longer rutting season is getting into full swing in some areas of the Deep South.

As their testosterone levels drop, the necks of the bucks go down in size, and shortly thereafter their antlers are cast. Most bucks lose their antlers from mid-December through to the end of January. We have a unique situation in northwestern New Jersey whereby many of our mature bucks cast their antlers during the first week in December. I once saw a dominant buck in Hunterdon County, New Jersey, that had cast one antler on November 25 and cast the other two days later. This antler casting is the earliest I have personally seen. The condition could be a genetic characteristic, but I am inclined to believe that it was partially caused by the sheer exhaustion of the mature bucks.

New Jersey's main hunting season always opened around December 5 to 7, after the main rut was over, and for years we had very few mature bucks. About 80 percent of our bucks are killed when they are seven-

Above: *The timing of the actual casting of a buck's antlers is determined by many factors. This buck has just lost his antlers. (Leonard Lee Rue III)*

Facing page: *For most of the bucks over the northern two-thirds of the United States, the rutting season is over when the swelling in their necks goes down. (Len Rue, Jr.)*

teen to eighteen months old. Without a balanced herd that contains a healthy proportion of mature bucks, the breeding season is chaotic, which places a great stress upon the entire herd, bucks and does alike. There is more chasing by all of the deer, resulting in fewer chances to rest and to feed at a time when weight and fat accumulation are critical to survival. Dominant bucks typically lose 20 to 25 percent of their body weight by the time the rut is over in mid-December. If the weather has stayed mild, the deer can still move about easily with a chance of obtaining food and regaining some of the lost weight. An early winter, starting in November, precludes this weight gain. An early winter sends the northernmost deer into their yards early. Deer that lose between 30 to 35 percent of their body weight die.

The hunting season is usually in full swing in most states in December, creating further stress in the deer and preventing them from feeding in the daylight hours.

Around December 15, if the temperature has lowered gradually, the bucks are dealt another blow. All deer's basic metabolism slows down. With the lowered metabolism, the bucks are not capable of eating as much as they could, or should, even if the food were available. Their daily intake is reduced to only 30 to 40 percent of what they would normally eat. I strongly suspect that it is the gradual lowering of the buck's metabolic rate that is inextricably linked to photoperiodism and that together they shut down the buck's testosterone level, ending the rut.

The deer's winter coat has grown to full length by early November, providing the deer with insulation that will allow it to easily withstand extreme cold. So little body heat is lost that the snow does not melt on the deer's back, and, if the deer lies still, the snow may

Above: *Adult deer can withstand extreme cold, but they cannot tolerate strong wind. (Leonard Lee Rue III)*

Left: *The long, hollow guard hair and the woolly undercoat provide the deer with excellent insulation. The deer does not give off enough body heat to melt the snow. (Leonard Lee Rue III)*

pile up several inches in depth. The deer cannot stand wind, and in the northern deer ranges they will seek out protected areas of dense cover and yard up. If not prohibited from doing so by hunting pressure, the deer will restrict their activities during the the long winter nights, feeding and moving only in the daylight hours when the temperature rises.

I have found that deer that are not molested tend to decrease their daily activity when the temperature drops to between twenty-eight and twenty-six degrees Fahrenheit. I have found that this same low temperature causes raccoons and skunks to den up. This lowered metabolic rate is a form of dormancy, providing a tremendous survival factor. When all of these actions, voluntary and involuntary, have been taken, the deer are as prepared to face the winter as they can be. That our deer population is increasing despite the winter and other hardships the deer encounter proves once again their great adaptability.

POSTSCRIPT

As I said in my introduction, I have written this book to share the new knowledge that I have learned since I updated my book *The Deer of North America* in 1989. I finished this new book on April 3, 1999—or at least I thought I had.

I have a two-and-one-half-year-old captive doe that I did not want bred and so kept her penned separately since the previous October. My big buck dropped his antlers in January. On April 1, I turned the doe back in with the herd, and, on April 8, the buck bred her. This April breeding means that the doe definitely came into estrus for six complete cycles. It also means that, although the buck's testosterone levels had dropped and his antlers had been cast, he still was able to copulate with her, six months after the peak of the breeding season.

The fawn was born October 23, which proves that the buck still had viable sperm. It also illustrates that, although the average gestation period for whitetails is 203 to 205 days, she delivered in 198 days, because she wasn't stressed by winter.

This story points to what I have stressed repeatedly: Life is a constant learning process, and none of us know all there is to know about anything. That is why I am planning to write another book on deer in 2009 and pass on to you all the new knowledge about deer that I know I'm going to learn in the next ten years.

Although the rutting season is over and his neck is no longer swollen, this buck is still capable of breeding. (Len Rue, Jr.)

BIBLIOGRAPHY

Ackerman, Diane. *A Natural History of the Senses*. New York: Random House, 1990.

Alsheimer, Charles J. *Whitetail: Behavior Through the Seasons*. Iola, Wis.: Krause Publications, 1996.

Atkeson, Thomas O., R. Larry Marchinton, and Karl V. Miller. "Vocalizations of White-Tailed Deer." *The American Midland Naturalist*. Vol. 120, No. 1, July 1988, p. 194–200.

Bailey, James A. *Principles of Wildlife Management*. New York: John Wiley & Sons, 1984.

Bauer, Erwin. *Deer in Their World*. Harrisburg, Pa.: Outdoor Life Books, 1983.

———. *Whitetails: Behavior, Ecology, Conservation*. Stillwater, Minn.: Voyageur Press, Inc., 1993.

Brown, Robert D., ed. *Antler Development in Cervidae*. Kingsville, Tex.: Texas A&M University, 1983.

———, ed. *The Biology of Deer*. New York: Springer-Verlag, 1992.

Bubenik, G. A., A. B. Bubenik, G. M. Brown, and D. A. Wilson. "Sexual Stimulation and Variations of Plasma Testosterone in Normal, Antiandrogen and Antiestrogen Treated White-tailed Deer (*Odocoileus virginianus*) During the Annual Cycle." *The Wildlife Society*. XIII International Congress of Game Biologists: p. 377–386.

Chepko-Sade, B. Diane and Zuleyma Tang Halpin, eds. *Mammalian Dispersal Patterns*. Chicago: The University of Chicago Press, 1987.

Clark, Mertice M. and Bennett G. Galef, Jr. "Where the Males Are." *Natural History*, November 1998, p. 14–22.

Cox, Daniel J. *Whitetail Country: The Photographic Life History of Whitetail Deer*. Text by John Ozoga. Wautoma, Wis.: Willow Creek Press, 1988.

Ehrenkranz, Joel R. L. "A Gland for All Seasons." *Natural History*, June 1983, p. 18–23.

Eisenberg, John F. and Devra G. Kleiman, eds. *Advances in the Study of Mammalian Behavior*. The American Society of Mammalogists. Special Publication #7, March 11, 1983.

Forsyth, Adrian. *A Natural History of Sex*. Shelburne, Vt.: Chapters Publishing Ltd., 1986.

Geist, Valerius. *Deer of the World: Their Evolution, Behavior & Ecology*. Mechanicsburg, Pa.: Stackpole Books, 1998.

Goss, Richard J. *Deer Antlers: Regeneration, Function and Evolution*. New York: Academic Press, Harcourt, Brace, Jovanovich, 1983.

Grzimek, Dr.; Dr. H. C. Bernhard, Editor-in-Chief. *Grizmek's Encyclopedia of Ethology*. New York: Van Nostrand Reinhold Company, 1977.

Halls, Lowell K., compiler and ed. *White-tailed Deer: Ecology and Management*. A Wildlife Management Institute Book. Harrisburg, Pa.: Stackpole Books, 1984.

Jacobson, Harry A. "Relationships Between Deer and Soil Nutrients in Mississippi." Wildlife Session, Annual Conference of South Eastern Association of Fish and Wildlife Agencies 38, p. 1–12.

Jacobson, Harry A., David C. Guynn, Jr., Robert N. Griffin, and Donald Lewis. "Fecundity of White-tailed Deer in Mississippi and Periodicity of Corpora Lutea and Lactation." Annual Conference of South Eastern Association of Fish and Wildlife Agencies 33, p. 30–35.

Johnson, Dr. Mark K. "Watching the Whitetail." *Safari*, May/June 1998, p. 14–16.

Kroll, Dr. James C. *A Practical Guide to Producing and Harvesting White-tailed Deer*. Nacogdoches, Tex.: Stephen F. Austin State University, 1991.

Leberg, Paul L. and Michael H. Smith. "Influence of Density on Growth of White-tailed Deer." *Journal of Mammalogy*. Vol. 74, No. 6, August 1993, p. 723–731.

Lingle, S. "Escape Gaits of White-tailed Deer, Mule Deer and Their Hybrids: Gaits Observed and Patterns of Limb Coordination." *Behaviour*. Vol. 122, p. 153–181.

MacDonald, D. W., D. Muller-Schwarze, and S. E. Natynczuk. *Chemical Signals in Vertebrates 5*. New York: Oxford University Press, 1990.

McFarland, David, ed. *The Oxford Companion to Animal Behavior*. New York: Oxford University Press, 1982.

McShea, William J., H. Brian Underwood, and John H. Rappole, eds. *The Science of Overabundance: Deer Ecology and Population Management.* Washington, D.C.: Smithsonian Institution Press, 1997.

Marchinton, R. Larry, Karl V. Miller, R. Joseph Hamilton, and David C. Guynn "Quality Deer Management: Biological and Social Impacts on the Herd." *Proceedings Tall Timbers Game Bird Seminar*, Tallahassee, Fla., March 9, 1990, p. 7–15.

Marchinton, R. Larry, Karen L. Johansen, and Karl V. Miller. "Behavioural Components of White-Tailed Deer Scent Marking: Social and Seasonal Effects." *Chemical Signals in Vertebrates* 5. New York: Oxford University Press, 1990, p. 295–301.

Meredith, M. "Sensory Processing in the Main and Accessory Olfactory Systems: Comparisons and Contrasts." *Journal of Steroid Biochemistry & Molecular Biology*, vol. 39 no. 4B, 1991, p. 601–614.

Miller, Karl V., R. Larry Marchinton and W. Matt Knox. "White-tailed Deer Signposts and Their Role as a Source of Priming Pheromones: A Hypothesis." *XVIII Congress of the International Union of Game Biologists*, Krakow, Poland, August 23–29, 1987, p. 1–8.

Miller, Karl V., R. Larry Marchinton, Kenneth J. Forand, and Karen L. Johansen. "Dominance, Testosterone Levels, and Scraping Activity in a Captive Herd of White-tailed Deer." *Journal of Mammalogy*, vol. 68, no. 4, November 1987, p. 812–817.

Miller, Karl V., R. Larry Marchinton, and Parshall B. Bush. "Signpost Communication by White-tailed Deer: Research Since Calgary." *Applied Animal Behaviour Science*, vol. 29, 1991, p. 195–204.

Miller, Karl V. and R. Larry Marchinton, eds. *Quality Whitetails.* Mechanicsburg, Pa.: Stackpole Books, 1995.

Nelson, Richard. *Heart and Blood: Living With Deer in America.* New York: Vintage Books, 1997.

Ozoga, John J. "Chemistry of Communicating." *Whitetails Unlimited Magazine*, Fall/Winter 1997, p. 13–16.

———. *Whitetail Autumn: Seasons of the Whitetail, Book One.* Minocqua, Wis.: Willow Creek Press, 1994.

———. *Whitetail Winter: Seasons of the Whitetail, Book Two.* Minocqua, Wis.: Willow Creek Press, 1995.

———. *Whitetail Spring: Seasons of the Whitetail, Book Three.* Minocqua, Wis.: Willow Creek Press, 1996.

———. *Whitetail Summer: Seasons of the Whitetail, Book Four.* Minocqua, Wis.: Willow Creek Press, 1997.

Ozoga, John J. and Louis J. Verme. "Comparative Breeding Behavior and Performance of Yearling vs. Prime-age White-tailed Bucks." *Journal of Wildlife Management*, vol. 49, no. 2, p. 364–372.

Ozoga, John J. and Louis J. Verme. "Relation of Maternal Age to Fawn-Rearing Success in White-tailed Deer." *Journal of Wildlife Management.* vol. 50, no. 3, p. 480–486.

Petersen, David. *Racks.* Santa Barbara, Calif.: Capra Press, 1991.

Putnam, Rory. *The Natural History of Deer.* Ithaca, NY: Comstock Publishing Associates, Cornell University Press, 1988.

Rayner, Claire, contributing ed. *Atlas of the Body.* New York: Rand McNally and Company, 1976.

Richardson, Larry W., Harry A. Jacobson, Robert J. Muncy, and Carroll J. Perkins. "Acoustics of White-tailed Deer (*Odocoileus Virginianus*)." *Journal of Mammalogy*, vol. 64, no. 2, 1983, p. 245–252.

Rue, Dr. Leonard Lee III. *The Deer of North America.* Danbury, Conn.: Outdoor Life Books, 1989.

———. *Whitetails.* Harrisburg, Pa.: Stackpole Books, 1991.

———. *The World of the White-tailed Deer.* New York: J. B. Lippincott Company, 1962.

Sherman, Paul W. and John Alcock, eds. *Exploring Animal Behavior: Readings from American Scientist, 2nd edition.* Sunderland, Mass.: Sinauer Associates, Inc., 1998.

Shorey, H. H. *Animal Communication by Pheromones.* New York: Academic Press, Harcourt, Brace, Jovanovich, 1976.

Suttie, James M. and Peter Fennessy. "Recent Advances in the Physiological Control of Velvet Antler Growth." *Biology of Deer.* New York: Springer-Verlag, 1992.

Von Besser, Kurt. *How Game Animals See & Smell.* Orangeburg, S.C.: Atsko/Sno-Seal, Inc., 1993.

Vroon, Piet. *The Secret Seducer: Smell.* New York: Farrar, Straus and Giroux, 1994.

Walther, Fritz, R. *Communication and Expression in Hoofed Mammals.* Bloomington, Ind.: Indiana University Press, 1984.

INDEX

Overleaf: *The sun may be going down on these whitetail bucks, but their future in our tomorrow is bright. (Leonard Lee Rue III)*

ABOUT
THE AUTHOR

(Photograph by Len Rue, Jr.)

Leonard Lee Rue III has spent much of his life studying, photographing, and living with wildlife in its natural habitats. The most published wildlife photographer in North America, he also is the author of twenty-six books on wildlife, including *How I Photograph Wildlife* and *The Deer of North America*, and he writes monthly columns for *Deer & Deer Hunting* and *Outdoor Photographer* magazines. He received the 1987 Outdoor Writers Association of America's "Excellence in Craft" Award. In 1990 he received an Honorary Doctorate of Science from Colorado State University, for "the dissemination of knowledge on wildlife," and in 1997 he received a Lifetime Achievement Award from the North American Nature Photographers' Association (NANPA).

In addition to his work as a writer and photographer, Dr. Rue conducts many lectures and seminars on white-tailed deer, turkey, and nature photography throughout the country each year. He also produces photographic, instructional, educational, and nature videos.

Dr. Rue and his wife, Uschi, own and operate Leonard Rue Video Productions, Inc., which supplies top-quality video footage covering the complete realm of wildlife and nature subjects. With his son, Len Rue, Jr., Dr. Rue also owns Leonard Rue Enterprises, a company that includes Leonard Rue Enterprises Stock Photo Agency and the L. L. Rue Catalog.

Leonard Rue Enterprises Stock Photo Agency supplies top-quality wildlife and nature photography, both color transparencies and black-and-white prints, to advertising and editorial markets worldwide.

The L. L. Rue Catalog offers a unique line of photographic equipment and accessories for the discriminating photographer and outdoor enthusiast. To receive a catalog, contact Leonard Rue Enterprises, 138 Millbrook Road, Blairstown, NJ 07825-9534, 1-800-734-2568, or rue@rue.com. For more information, visit www.rue.com.